Sherlock Holmes

Sherlock Holmes

In His Own Words and in the
Words of Those Who Knew Him

Edited by Barry Day

TAYLOR TRADE PUBLISHING
Lanham • New York • Oxford

First Taylor Trade Publishing edition 2003

This Taylor Trade Publishing hardcover edition of *Sherlock Holmes: In His Own Words and in the Words of Those Who Knew Him* is an original publication. It is published by arrangement with the editor.

Published by Taylor Trade Publishing
A Member of the Rowman & Littlefield Publishing Group
4501 Forbes Blvd., Suite 200
Lanham, Maryland 20706

Distributed by National Book Network

Library of Congress Cataloging-in-Publication Data

Sherlock Holmes : in his own words and in the words of those who knew him / edited by Barry Day.
p. cm.
Includes index.
ISBN 0-87833-297-9 (alk. paper)
1. Doyle, Arthur Conan, Sir, 1859–1930—Characters—Sherlock Holmes.
2. Detective and mystery stories, English—History and criticism.
3. Holmes, Sherlock (Fictitious character) 4. Private investigators in literature. I. Day, Barry.

PR4624 .S474 2003
823'.8—dc21
2002154598

⊗™ The paper used in this publication meets the minimum requirements of American National Standard for Information Sciences—Permanence of Paper for Printed Library Materials, ANSI/NISO Z39.48–1992.
Manufactured in the United States of America.

To Sir Arthur Conan Doyle

Only those things the heart *believes* are true . . .

A yellow fog swirls past the window-pane
As night descends upon this fabled street:
A lonely hansom splashes through the rain,
And ghostly gas lamps fail at twenty feet.
Here, though the world explode, these two survive,
And it is always eighteen ninety-five.

—Vincent Starrett

"The Return of Sherlock Holmes." (Frederic Dorr Steele, 1903)

Contents

Introduction

"'Come, Watson, come!' he cried. 'The game is afoot.'"

—"The Abbey Grange"

I T SURPRISES many people to learn that more has been written about Sherlock Holmes and Doctor Watson in one century than about Shakespeare in four. In fact, what should surprise is that so much has been written about someone who couldn't even decide how to spell his own name.

Holmes and Watson fascinate us endlessly because they represent the two sides of each of us. Holmes is the superman we would like to be; Watson the decent, down to earth soul we know ourselves to be. The strain of being *all* Holmes would be too great; the limitation of being *only* Watson not sufficiently satisfying to our ego. But the sum of the *parts*. . . .

In studying their life together it's fascinating to see how their mutual interdependence evolves. At first Watson is the sorcerer's apprentice, totally enthralled and happy to bring up the rear, take notes and do whatever is required. But later—and intermittently—he has a life of his own, which Holmes does not.

Watson marries—at least twice—and leaves Baker Street for periods of time and, although he always seems glad to be back, it is invariably Holmes who initiates his return. As the years go by—as is so often the case—the balance of the relationship changes and by the turn of the century it is Holmes who is the more dependent of the two. Holmes who has to winkle Watson out of his practice to accompany him on some adventure or another. In "The Mazarin Stone" we are told of "the gaps of loneliness and isolation that surrounded the saturnine figure of the great detective."

Without Watson there would have *been* no Holmes. (How much would we know of Dr. Johnson if there had been no Boswell?) But Watson was infinitely more than a sympathetic and honest biographer; he was his friend's touchstone—or, more properly, his *whetstone*. He kept Holmes sharp.

Holmes admitted that he liked to talk his cases through as they progressed. ("Nothing clears up a case so much as stating it to another person") and he would test his hypotheses on Watson, in the knowledge that Watson would bring no preconceptions to bear. His reactions were truly instinctive and he had no desire to compete. "I am here to serve, Holmes." . . . Holmes found him "invaluable as a companion."

Certainly the cleverer and opinionated Holmes patronized him in the early years but as those years went by, he developed a respect as well as a genuine affection for his companion. The concern he shows for Watson's physical safety in later cases such as "The Devil's Foot" and "The Three Garridebs" made evident a depth of emotion that Watson found both surprising and gratifying. Though neither of them would ever have used it, 'love' was the word that best summed up the bond that grew between them and, although Holmes always claimed that his Bible knowledge was "rusty," he would certainly have seen the relevance of the quotation—"Greater love hath no man than this, that a man lay down his life for his friends" (John 15:13). Whenever the game was afoot, it was tacitly understood that each was prepared to do just that for the other.

Holmes himself was a living contradiction. He claimed to distrust emotion ("Whatever is emotional is opposed to that true, cold reason which I place above all things"), yet he is constantly doing things which smack of the knight errant. ("I had a glimpse of a great heart as well as a great brain.")

He belittles Watson's literary efforts ("those narratives with which you have afflicted a long-suffering public"), yet tacitly encourages them, for the very good reason that he needs the 'advertising' they provide. The vast majority of his cases, it must be remembered, ended up with the official police force being given the credit for solving them. To promote his reputation Holmes needed Watson and his "attempts which I had made to give publicity to (his) methods." All of which ended with his retirement— as Watson duly records . . . "So long as he was in actual professional practice the records of his successes were of some practical value to him; but since he has definitely retired from London . . . notoriety has become hateful to him, and he has peremptorily requested that his wishes in this matter should be strictly observed." Note the use of "peremptorily." One wonders if his attitude would have differed had Watson offered him a share of the royalties.

Watson's role as both interpreter to and insulation from the rest of the world was not the least of his contributions to the legend of Sherlock Holmes.

* * * *

Soon after they meet, Watson attempts an analysis of his eccentric friend's eclectic skills. In most cases he hopelessly underestimated Holmes's knowledge and accomplishments—even though it can be argued that Holmes, that "omnivorous reader"—was constantly learning and improving his mind. Nor did he feel any obligation to let Watson know what new matter he might be adding and storing in that "little box-room" he called a mind.

The mature Holmes was truly a Renaissance man with a breadth of knowledge and—more importantly—the ability to draw connections between what he knew, which would provide new insights. Unique among his profession, he had the ability to focus totally on the matter in hand and strip away the layers of irrelevance until he had defined the essence of a problem.

Of course, he lived in the last possible age when omniscience in an individual remained a possibility. It can be argued that in this computer age of in-depth specialism Holmes would have found no place—but this, I feel, is to miss the point about the man. The essential skill of Sherlock Holmes lay in understanding what something *meant*. In an age when we have so much information, so many 'clues,' we have an even greater need for a man who understands the meaning of the matter. One can just see him by that same fireside updating his index on his laptop and e-mailing for information from his contacts round the world.

Certainly he codified the art (or science) of detection and added dimension to it from both the technological and psychological point of view. For that alone he would deserve to be remembered. But the man was a humanitarian, too. Time and again, he took it upon himself to be the "court of final appeal" and temper justice with mercy. In a society and at a time that turned a blind eye to inequality, his covert influence at every level in that society did something to help balance the scales, even though we may never know the full extent of his contribution. Even Watson was never allowed to know that.

Many lesser men died laden with greater honors but few are as alive today in so many hearts as Mr. Sherlock Holmes, late of Baker Street and Sussex—and that is its own kind of immortality.

Note

Since Watson published the last of his cases in 1927 we have seen the publication of a great deal of Sherlockian scholarship of varying quality. *Sherlock Holmes: In His Own Words* attempts to do just what the title suggests—allow Holmes to tell his own story in his own words (and, of course, those of Watson.) Since he never attempted a formal autobiography—although his intended history of detection would undoubtedly have contained elements of one—there will necessarily be gaps the reader will have to fill in for himself or herself. In such cases, it is as well to remember the Master's key axiom that when you have eliminated the impossible.

As any student of Holmes is well aware, Dr. Watson was notoriously inconsistent with his dating of cases and events. The date of publication clearly has no relation to the date of the case itself. When Watson does not specify in the text, I have tried, as far as possible, to refer to a case by the date when it is *generally* thought by Holmes scholars to have taken place, and the sequence of events described uses that chronology as a basis.

BARRY DAY
April 2003

"Young Stamford"

"He's a walking calendar of crime ... You'll find him a knotty problem, though. I'll wager he learns more about you than you about him."

—Stamford in *A Study in Scarlet*

MOST OF WHAT we know about Sherlock Holmes is derived from the accounts of his friend, collaborator, and 'Boswell'—Dr. John H. Watson. In only three of the sixty adventures does Holmes narrate his own story and even then it is clear that he is surprisingly self-conscious. Despite his many criticisms of Watson as a romanticizer of events, picking up his own pen gives Holmes a grudging admiration for the doctor's literary skills. He did not make a habit of it.

He first appeared in Watson's life like the character in a Shakespearean play, his entrance heralded by a minor character—in this case Young Stamford. Stamford had been a dresser under Watson during a period at St. Bartholomew's Hospital in London where Watson was a staff surgeon in the early 1870s.

Returned from the second Afghan War, his health and finances severely depleted, Watson finds himself at a loss as to what to do next . . .

"I had neither kith nor kin in England, and was, therefore, as free as air—or as free as an income of eleven shillings and sixpence a day (his army pension) will permit a man to be. Under such circumstances I naturally gravitated to London, that great cesspool into which all the loungers and idlers of the Empire are irresistibly drained. There I stayed at a private hotel in the Strand, leading a comfortless, meaningless existence, and spending such money as I had, considerably more freely than I ought." (A *Study in Scarlet*)

By early January 1881 he decides it is time to make a move to cheaper lodgings. On the day he makes his decision he is standing in the bar at the Criterion when he feels a tap on the shoulder and turns to find Stamford. The two of them had never been close in the old days but changed circumstances make them particularly pleased to see one another. Before long they are reminiscing over lunch at the Holborn.

When Watson mentions his need to share accommodation, Stamford remarks that this is the second time that day someone has discussed that very subject with him—the first being "a fellow who is working at the chemical laboratory up at the hospital."

"He was bemoaning himself this morning because he could not get someone to go halves with him in some nice rooms he had found, and which were too much for his purse."

Watson declares himself to be anxious to meet this man. The arrangement sounds ideal. "I should prefer having a partner to being alone."

At which Stamford observes predictively—"You don't know Sherlock Holmes yet, perhaps you would not care for him as a constant companion."

Questioned by Watson, he elaborates:

"He is a little queer in his ideas—an enthusiast in some branches of science . . . I have no idea what he intends to go in for. I believe he is well up in anatomy, and he is a first-class chemist; but, as far as I know, he has never taken out any systematic medical classes. His studies are very desultory and eccentric, but he has amassed a lot of out-of-the-way knowledge which would astonish his professors. He is not a man that is easy to draw out, though he can be communicative enough when the fancy seizes him . . . He either avoids the laboratory for weeks or else he works there from morning to night."

Stamford offers to introduce Watson to Holmes at the laboratory but on the way there feels compelled to keep himself at arm's length from the outcome. Watson senses the reservation and questions it.

"It's not easy to express the inexpressible," Stamford answers. "Holmes is a little too scientific for my tastes—it approaches to cold-bloodedness. I could imagine his giving a friend a little pinch of the latest vegetable alkaloid, not out of malevolence, you understand, but simply out of a spirit of enquiry in order to have an accurate idea of the effects. To do him justice, I think that he would take it himself with the same readiness. He appears to have a passion for definite and exact knowledge . . . but it may be pushed to excess. When it comes to beating subjects in the dissecting-rooms with a stick . . . to verify how far bruises may be produced after death . . . it is certainly taking rather a bizarre shape . . . Heaven knows what the objects of his studies are."

They arrive at the laboratory, "a lofty chamber, lined and littered with countless bottles. Broad, low tables were scattered about, which bristled with retorts, test-tubes, and little Bunsen lamps, with their blue flickering flames. There was only one student in the room, who was bending over a distant table absorbed in his work."

It was the first time Watson was to see the man who would share and change such a large part of his life. And the first words he heard from Holmes's lips were—"I've found it! I've found it! I have found a re-agent which is precipitated by haemoglobin, and by nothing else." In the test tube brandished by this wild-eyed stranger— Watson was to learn later—was "the most practical medico-legal discovery for years . . . an infallible test for blood stains."

Stepping into the breach—and effecting the most historic introduction since Stanley's "Dr. Livingstone, I presume"— Stamford says . . .

"Dr. Watson, Mr. Sherlock Holmes."

"'How are you?' he said cordially, gripping my hand with a strength for which I should hardly have given him credit. 'You have been in Afghanistan, I perceive.'"

The following day this odd couple moved into rooms at 221b Baker Street—and the game was afoot.

"I've found it! I have found a re-agent which is precipitated by haemo-globin, and by nothing else." Young Stamford introduces his friend, Dr. John H. Watson, to Sherlock Holmes at St. Bart's Hospital. (George Hutchinson for *A Study in Scarlet*, 1891).

221b: "Some Nice Rooms"

"I have my eye on a suite in Baker Street which
would suit us down to the ground. You don't mind
the smell of strong tobacco, I hope?"

—A Study in Scarlet

THE SUITE "consisted of a couple of comfortable bedrooms and a single large airy sitting-room cheerfully furnished, and illuminated by two broad windows (one of them a bow window). So desirable in every way were the apartments, and so moderate did the terms seem when divided between us, that the bargain was concluded upon the spot, and we at once entered into possession. That very evening (Watson records) I moved my things round from the hotel and on the following morning Sherlock Holmes followed me with several boxes and portmanteaus."

[The designation 221b was presumably based on the French "*bis*," indicating a subdivision of the primary residence.]

For the next twenty-two years on and off this would be their home with Watson taking the occasional marital sabbatical and

Holmes an enforced three-year absence during the Great Hiatus of 1891–1894 caused by Professor Moriarty. Watson, in retrospect, considered Holmes "the very worst tenant in London. On the other hand, his payments were princely (£4 a week). I have no doubt that the house might have been purchased at the price which Holmes paid for his rooms during the years that I was with him."

Contrary to many subsequent depictions, Baker Street, NW1 was perfectly straight and 221b situated on the west side of it. When Holmes returned 'from the dead' and was anticipating an assassination attempt from Moriarty's only remaining lieutenant, Colonel Sebastian Moran ("the second most dangerous man in London"), he expects it to come from Camden House, since it stands immediately opposite to 221b. Because the location is so precise, Holmes and Watson are able to locate the back door of the empty premises precisely ("The Empty House") and ambush the ambusher.

Architecturally, Baker Street at that time seems to have been relatively uninspiring. At the opening of *The Sign of Four* Holmes—contemplating a typical London 'pea-souper'—invites Watson to "Stand at the window here. Was ever such a dreary, dismal, unprofitable world? See how the yellow fog swirls down the streets and drifts across the dun-coloured houses. What could be more hopelessly prosaic and material?" On another occasion he stands "at the parted blinds, gazing into the dull, neutral-tinted London street."

"On a bleak autumnal morning" in 1886 ("The Noble Bachelor") they were both content to sit "after breakfast on either side of a cheery fire in the old room"—their traditional places—as "a thick fog rolled down between the lines of dun-coloured houses," and they were still sitting there in 1894 before the adventure of "The Golden Pince-Nez," as outside "the occasional lamps gleamed on the expanse of muddy road and shining pavement," while "the wind howled and screamed at the windows."

A year later—perhaps influenced by the dire threat of the loss of "The Bruce-Partington Plans"—"a dense brown fog" made it "impossible to see from our windows the loom of the opposite houses . . . the greasy brown swirl drifting past and condensing into oily drops upon the window-panes."

The area, however, shared the mood swings of its most famous resident. In September 1889 during the affair of "The Cardboard Box"—"Baker Street was like an oven, and the glare of the sunlight upon the yellow brickwork of the house across the road (presumably Camden House) was painful to the eye. It was hard to believe that these were the same walls which loomed so gloomily through the fogs of winter."

Behind the house there appears to have been a small enclosed garden of no great beauty. In October 1900—at the time of the Thor Bridge affair—Watson was dressing in his bedroom (on the second floor and presumably facing the back) and notes that it was "a wild morning . . . the last remaining leaves were being whirled from the solitary plane tree which graces the yard behind our house."

* * * *

As far as the interior layout was concerned, it is likely that—according to Victorian custom—the owner of the house (the widow, Mrs. Hudson) would have retained the whole of the ground floor for her personal use and rented Holmes and Watson most of the top two floors.

On the first floor—in America the second floor—was the communal sitting room, which contained the door to Holmes's bedroom. In "The Mazarin Stone" (1903) we learn that the bedroom has another door—presumably to the corridor—since Holmes is able to double back and surprise his visitors. ("I think we will go out through the bedroom. This second exit is exceedingly use-ful.") Watson's own quarters were on the floor above, since he refers to coming *down* to breakfast. Mrs. Hudson may also have been on the same floor with any occasional cook or maid on the third floor.

In the same story reference is made to "the waiting room at 221b." This is somewhat puzzling. In the majority of the adventures the client is shown straight up the stairs to the living-room—on several occasions Holmes and Watson arrive home to find someone *in situ*—but presumably there were occasions when Mrs. Hudson would press her best ground-floor parlor into tem-porary service.

"The sharp clang of the bell" was the cue that another adven-ture was about to begin . . .

"Now is the dramatic moment of fate, Watson, when you hear a step upon the stair which is walking into your life, and you know not whether for good or ill." (*The Hound of the Baskervilles*)

Even the *way* it clanged was enough to provide Holmes with some of the data he craved. As he told Watson in "A Case of Identity"—"Oscillation upon the pavement always means an *affaire du coeur.*"

*   *   *   *

In addition to their living quarters, Holmes and Watson rented several lumber rooms, presumably on the floor above. In "The Six Napoleons" Holmes goes into "one of the lumber rooms" to search through his collection of the back copies of the daily newspapers "with which (it) was packed."

Filing and finding a particular back issue must have pre-sented problems, since Holmes's tidy mind was not reflected in his treatment of the daily press. Watson would often come down

221b . . . the Sitting Room.

to breakfast to find "a pile of crumpled morning papers, evidently newly studied."

Late Victorian London offered a vastly greater choice of periodicals than we have today. Watson was a regular reader of the morning *Daily Chronicle*—as well as the *Sporting Times* when he was in a betting mood—while Holmes favored the *Daily Gazette* for its crime news. He would also use the *Evening News*, the *Evening Standard*, the *Pall Mall Gazette*, the *St. James's Gazette*, the *Star, Echo,* and the *Globe* when he needed to advertise for one reason or another.

He could—and often did—also make use of *The Times*, the *Morning Post*, the *Daily News*, and the *Daily Herald*. ("*The Times* is a paper which is seldom found in any hands but those of the highly educated."—*The Valley of Fear*)

Naturally, it was his favorite; Watson preferred the *Telegraph*.

Holmes often insisted—perhaps too much so—that his reading of Fleet Street's finest was severely restricted—"I read nothing except the criminal news and the agony columns . . . What a chorus of groans, cries and bleatings! What a rag-bag of singular happenings! . . . But surely the most valuable hunting-ground that ever was given to a student of the unusual." ("The Red Circle")

"The Press, Watson, is a most valuable institution if you only know how to use it." ("The Six Napoleons")

* * * *

It would also have been quite likely that he may have rented other storage space for the host of miscellaneous material he found germane to his profession, and many students have speculated that Mrs. Hudson's cellar may have been devoted to an overflow laboratory to house Holmes's more ambitious experiments.

Precisely how the rooms evolved to their mature state is not recorded but when all the artifacts were in place we have firm evidence of the following:

. . . a dining table and chairs, together with a sideboard ("he cut a slice of beef from the joint upon the sideboard") for breakfast and other meals . . . the two large armchairs on either side of the fireplace sacrosanct to the tenants (Watson on the left of the fireplace) . . . at least one comfortable visitor's "basket" chair ("It is my habit to sit with my back to the window and to place my visitors in the opposite chair, where the light falls full upon them . . . I have found it wise to impress my clients with a sense of power."—"The Blanched Soldier"). In "The Five Orange Pips" Holmes "turns the lamp away from himself and towards the vacant chair upon which a newcomer must sit." There was also a sofa on which Holmes would lie and brood when bored. (". . . reactions of lethargy during which he would lie about with his violin and his books, hardly moving save from the sofa to the table."—"The Musgrave Ritual") In front of the fire was a "bearskin hearthrug." ("The Priory School")

Much of the rest of the room bore witness to Watson's claim that "in his personal habits (Holmes) was one of the most untidy men that ever drove a fellow-lodger to distraction . . . When I find a man who keeps his cigars in the coal-scuttle, his tobacco in the toe end of a Persian slipper, and his unanswered correspondence transfixed by a jack-knife into the very centre of his wooden mantlepiece, then I begin to give myself virtuous airs. I have always held, too, that pistol practice should be distinctly an open-air pastime; and when Holmes in one of his queer humours, would sit in an armchair with his hair-trigger and a hundred Boxer cartridges and proceed to adorn the opposite wall with a patriotic 'V.R.' done in bullet-pocks, I felt strongly that neither the atmosphere nor the appearance of our room was improved by it."

In one corner of the room was the "acid-stained, deal-topped table" on which he conducted the "weird and malodorous scientific experiments" that Watson so dreaded. ("A formidable array of bottles and test tubes told me he had spent his day in the chemical work that was so dear to him.") If Watson had been capable of both seeing and observing, he would have been warned at their first meeting by the sight of Holmes's hands, "mottled over with pieces of plaster, and discoloured with strong acids." In "The Musgrave Ritual" he complains that their "chambers were always full of chemicals and criminal relics, which had a way of wandering into unlikely positions, and of turning up in the butter-dish or in even less desirable places." There was also a spirit case and a gasogene—a device for creating aerated soda water.

In another corner leaned the violin case containing Holmes's beloved Stradivarius.

On each side of the fireplace were book shelves. Holmes's side contained his 'commonplace books,' the collection of scrapbooks that contained reference material on a wide range of people, places, and events ("which many of our fellow citizens would have been so glad to burn"). So complex were their contents that the volumes required a separate index and constant updating. Holmes clearly found this a chore. In "The Five Orange Pips" Watson records him sitting "moodily at one side of the fireplace cross-indexing his records of crime," while in "The Bruce-Partington Plans" he is also "cross-indexing his huge book of references" . . . "the record of old cases, mixed with the accumulated information of a lifetime."

"He had a horror of destroying documents, especially those which were connected with his past cases," Watson recalled, "and yet it was only once in every year or two that he would muster energy to docket and arrange them."

Time and again the effort proves worthwhile, for there are few items that prove to be more than a fingertip away when the occasion demands, and many of them keep strange company. When he first looks up Irene Adler, for instance, he finds her sandwiched—so to speak—between entries on "a Hebrew Rabbi (Adler) and a staff-commander who had written a monograph upon the deep-sea fishes."

"'Make a long arm, Watson, and see what V has to say . . .'

I leaned back and took down the great index volume to which he had referred. Holmes balanced it on his knee and his eyes moved slowly and lovingly over the record of old cases, mixed with accumulated information of a lifetime.

'Voyage of the Gloria Scott,' he read. 'That was a bad business . . . Victor Lynch, the forger. Venomous lizard or gila. Remarkable case that! Victoria, the circus belle. Vanderbilt and the Yeggman. Vipers. Vigor, the Hammersmith wonder . . . Good old index. You can't beat it . . .'" ("The Sussex Vampire")

The bookshelves also held "the long row of year-books which fill a shelf" and "the dispatch-cases filled with documents, a perfect quarry for the student, not only of crime, but of the social and official scandals of the late Victorian era." ("The Veiled Lodger") Somewhere squeezed in close to hand would be the *American Encyclopaedia*, *Crockford's Clerical Directory*, *Whitaker's Almanac* ("Though reserved in its earlier vocabulary, it became, if I remember right, quite garrulous towards the end"), and the invaluable *Bradshaw Railway Guide* ("the vocabulary of *Bradshaw* is nervous and terse but limited"), probably "on a shelf of the break-front bookcase between works on the manufacture of paper and a set of the Newgate calendar."

Somewhere near at hand was "the famous tin box which was half filled with bundles of papers tied separately with ribbon," containing

"Hullo! Hullo! Good old index. You can't beat it. Listen to this, Watson."
(Howard K. Elcock for "The Sussex Vampire," 1924)

notes on his cases, "all done prematurely before my biographer had come to glorify me."

"Without his scrapbooks, his chemicals, and his homely untidiness, he was an uncomfortable man." ("The Three Students")

The walls of the room were adorned at the time of "The Mazarin Stone" (1903) with "scientific charts," and ever after "A Scandal in Bohemia" with the portrait of Irene Adler in evening dress—"*The* woman" with "that beautiful, haunted face, the startled eyes." (Watson's description)

In "The Dying Detective" (1887) we see into Holmes's bedroom. The mantlepiece was "a litter of pipes, tobacco-pouches, syringes, penknives, revolver cartridges, and other debris" and every wall was "adorned" with "the pictures of celebrated criminals." It was fairly safe to assume that pride of place in that gallery would be accorded to Charles Peace (1832–1879). Holmes—who may even have known him—always commended that the murderer had a "complex mind . . . all great criminals have that." This particular one had something else to commend him to Holmes—"My old friend Charlie Peace was a violin virtuoso."

Watson's bedroom was on the floor above the sitting room. Little is recorded of his personal possessions except for the unframed portraits of his heroes—Henry Ward Beecher (1813–1887), the American preacher during the Civil War era, and General Sir Charles Gordon (1833–1885), the famous British soldier who was killed at Khartoum. They stood on top of a pile of his books, which must certainly have included a number of "Clark Russell's fine sea-stories," ("the prose Homer of the great ocean") as well as a selection of "yellow-backed novels" all of which presumably accompanied him to his various marital abodes, only to return intermittently to Baker Street. On one occasion we find him "skipping over the pages of Henri Murger's *Vie*

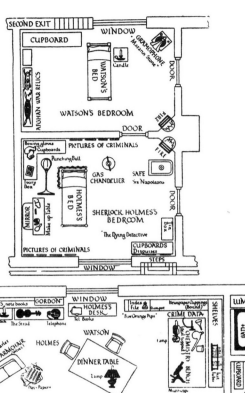

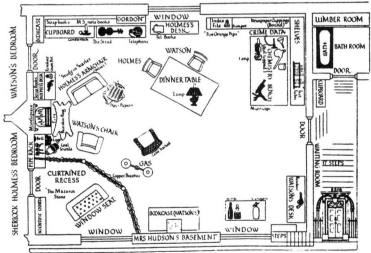

221b . . . the general layout.

de Bohème," presumably to brush up his "natural Bohemianism of disposition."

* * * *

During "the hour after breakfast" Holmes "was accustomed to deliver his opinions on the news of the day" and to read his "letters from a fishmonger and a tide-waiter," which caused him to remark lugubriously that "my correspondence has certainly the charm of variety and the humbler are usually the more interesting." ("The Noble Bachelor") . . . "I am somewhat on my guard against any packages which reach me." ("The Dying Detective.")

* * * *

While so much stayed the same over the years, innovation was allowed to creep in on a limited scale. In 1889 Holmes acquired the phonograph he was to use to such effect in "The Mazarin Stone" (1903), when he confuses his opponents into thinking they are listening to him playing the Hoffman Barcarolle on his violin when what they are hearing is a recording. ("These modern gramophones are a remarkable invention.")

The telephone arrived somewhat later—around 1898. It was used in the case of "The Retired Colourman" and we find Watson looking up the directory in "The Three Garridebs" (June 1901) as to the manner born.

"Thanks to the telephone and the help of the Yard, I can usually get my essentials without leaving this room."

Until then, when Holmes wished to communicate with the outside world, he rarely wrote a letter. Instead he made ample use of delivery services and, of course, the ubiquitous telegram.

(Twenty words for a shilling.) As Watson observed in "The Devil's Foot"— "Sherlock Holmes never writes when a telegram will do."

In the early years the rooms would certainly have been illuminated by gas, and since electricity was slow in coming to London, it is unlikely that 221b would have had anything but a limited supply until the turn of the century.

*   *   *   *

For most of their time in 221b their landlady was the trusty and much put upon Mrs. Martha Hudson, although there are one or two questions surrounding her tenure. Holmes and Watson move in in 1881 and Mrs. Hudson is mentioned in their first case (*A Study In Scarlet*) as well as "The Speckled Band" (1883), yet by the time of "A Scandal in Bohemia" (May 1887), Holmes refers to a 'Mrs. Turner' as their 'landlady.' Possibly the lady was a friend of Mrs. Hudson's and acting as a *locum* during one of her visits to her family, because she is never heard of again.

Much later—toward the end of 1900 at the time of the Thor Bridge affair—Holmes warns Watson about the "hard-boiled eggs with which our new cook has favoured us." Was Mrs. Hudson away again or—as is much more likely—was she now so comfortably off on the twenty years of rent that she felt she could afford to hire a cook and become a lady of comparative leisure herself? If so, it is unlikely that she escaped a comment similar to the one Holmes addressed to his friend on that occasion.

"The condition of the eggs may not be unconnected with the copy of the *Family Herald* which I observed yesterday upon the hall-table. Even so trivial a matter as cooking an egg demands an attention which is conscious of the passage of time, and incompatible with the love romance in that excellent periodical."

It seems unlikely that there was a repetition. Nobody—least of all Holmes and Watson—wants an outsider upsetting the even tenor of Baker Street routine.

Mrs. Hudson's "cuisine is a little limited, but she has as good an idea of breakfast as a Scotchwoman" ("The Naval Treaty") and when we hear that sharp clanging bell, it is her "stately tread" upon those seventeen stairs and none-other's that we expect to hear on the stair before she announces—"A gentleman to see you, Mr. Holmes . . ."

"We have had some dramatic entrances and exits upon our small stage at Baker Street." ("The Stockbroker's Clerk")

(In later years there seems to have been a page—or, more probably, a series of them. At least two of them were called Billy. By the time of the affair of "The Mazarin Stone" (1903) the current Billy was a "very wise and tactful page, who had helped a little to fill up the gaps of loneliness and isolation which surrounded the saturnine figure of the great detective"—Watson had married for the third time the previous year and moved to Queen Anne Street. It is not clear when he was employed but he refers to the events of "The Empty House" (1894) as being before his time. In any case, for Holmes to refer to him as "that boy" suggests someone in his teens.)

"Mrs. Hudson stood in the deepest awe of (Holmes)" (Watson observed in "The Dying Detective") and never dared to interfere with him, however outrageous his proceedings might seem. She was fond of him, too, for "he has a remarkable gentleness and courtesy in his dealings with women."

"Billy, the young but very wise and tactful page." (A. Gilbert for "The Mazarin Stone," 1921)

Her devotion was proved on more than one occasion, most specifically when she put herself at physical risk by moving the wax figure of Holmes around the lighted window of their sitting-room to confuse the would-be assassin in "The Empty Room."

What happened when Holmes retired to the Sussex Downs in 1903? It's possible that Mrs. Hudson remained in Baker Street and put up the "Rooms to Let" sign but it seems far more likely that she was the 'old housekeeper' Holmes refers to in "His Last Bow," who was still attending to his needs as late as 1914. To serve breakfast to some predictable office clerk after twenty years of expecting the unexpected would have been too much of an anti-climax.

"The Introspective Dreamer of Baker Street"

WE KNOW relatively little of Holmes before Baker Street. Occasionally Watson was able to quarry a nugget of fact from him and even more occasionally Holmes would offer something voluntarily, but it was in the nature of the man to be private in his personal life and he left no personal records.

"I had never heard him refer to his relations, and hardly ever to his own early life, and this reticence upon his past had increased the somewhat inhuman effect which he produced upon me," Watson wrote in "The Resident Patient." It was only at the time of the affair of "The Greek Interpreter" (September 1888) that Watson first learned that Holmes had an older brother, Mycroft—and by that time they had shared rooms for over seven years!

"My ancestors were country squires, who appear to have led much the same life as is natural to their class," he told Watson at the time—a remark that has led to speculation that there may have

Holmes by Sidney Paget (1904). This illustration was undiscovered and unpublished until 1951.

been other siblings. The tradition in middle and upper class Victorian families was to pass property on to the eldest son, leaving younger sons to enter the army and the Church, respectively.

Holmes found his own 'religion' and Mycroft—as we shall see—found his rather large niche in government service. Which raises the question—who succeeded to the Holmes estates? Was there a third and even older brother who, for some reason, is never mentioned—perhaps *because* he elected to do something so predictable and boring? And did the genes of family genius really pass him by or merely take a different turn?

There would seem to be a strong possibility that the "country squires" hailed from Sussex, since Holmes had that county in mind for his leisure years long before he actually retired there.

For want of other information, it must be assumed that Holmes passed his youth and adolescence in the family home, possibly with a private tutor. This would account for his familiarity with the way of country houses and perhaps for his distrust of country ways.

"It is one of the curses of mind with a turn like mine that I must look at everything with reference to my own special subject. You look at these scattered houses, and you are impressed by their beauty. I look at them, and the only thought which comes to me is a feeling of their isolation, and of the impunity with which crime may be committed there . . . It is my belief, founded on my experience, that the lowest and vilest alleys in London do not present a more dreadful record of sin than does the smiling and beautiful countryside." ("The Noble Bachelor")

He may at some point have visited the United States. Once again, he was to show knowledge of people and places there that must have preceded the Watson years or his biographer would surely have mentioned Holmes's later travels, had he known of them.

Some scholars have speculated that Holmes used the sabbatical years between university and St. Bart's to travel—specifically to the United States. One view is that he was employed as an actor, a profession which helped him acquire his subsequent skill with makeup and disguises. He must certainly have made friends in law enforcement. In "The Dancing Men" he calls in a professional IOU from his friend, Wilson Hargreaves of the New York Police 'Bureau' (*Department*), who had—according to Holmes—"more than once made use of my knowledge of London crime."

Is it not possible—indeed, likely—that in his quest to qualify himself for his chosen work Holmes would have made contact with Alan Pinkerton (1819–1884), founder of the famous Pinkerton Detective Agency and even worked for him, so as to learn state-of-the-art investigative techniques? Certainly, his admiration for Pinkerton's is obvious when he encounters Leverton, hero of the Long Island Cave Mystery in "The Red Circle."

In "The Noble Bachelor" Holmes waxes (for him) quite lyrical about the country as a whole.

It is hard to avoid the conclusion that Holmes had firsthand experience of the country by the casually knowledgeable way he refers to it and its ways. He recognizes the name of the "Pennsylvania Small Arms Company" as being a "well-known American firm" and says that "paying for brains" is the "American business principle." Not conclusive evidence, perhaps, but he seems to be identifying with them at a time when the average Englishman would have adopted a rather defensive third person stance towards 'them.'

"It is always a joy to meet an American . . . for I am one of those who believe that the folly of a monarch and the blundering of a Minister in far gone years will not prevent our children from being some day citizens of the same world-wide country under a flag which shall be the quartering of the Union Jack and the Stars and Stripes."

* * * *

He was almost certainly born in 1854 (probably on January 6), which would make him twenty-seven when he met Watson. In "His Last Bow" at the outbreak of World War I in 1914, he is sixty. Since Mycroft is seven years his senior, that puts his brother's birth year as 1847.

What is certain is that Holmes attended one of the two great universities—Oxford or Cambridge—but we are never told which. This may have been deliberate obfuscation on Holmes's part, since Watson is later to take care to hide the identities of the universities they visit in "The Three Students" and "The Creeping Man" by referring to 'Camford.' Holmes deliberately refers only to "the two years I was in college." Since he considered Cambridge an "inhospitable town" and was "effortlessly superior," I choose to believe he was at Oxford and a Balliol man!

The fact that he only stayed for two years, when most university courses took three or even four, suggests that he was impatient to get on with the work that was even then beginning to obsess him. Certainly he must have left without a degree. Supposing he went to university, as most students do, at, say, nineteen, he could not have been more than twenty-two when he came down—five years before that fateful encounter in the laboratory. Time to travel as well as study—or to travel as *part* of his studies.

At college he was predictably a loner. In his own first person telling of "The Gloria Scott" affair—his first case—he relates that "the only friend I ever made" there was one Victor Trevor.

(Although Reginald Musgrave was apparently also a college acquaintance. He was to bring Holmes one of his earliest and most intriguing cases with the riddle of "The Musgrave Ritual.") "I was never a very sociable fellow . . . always fond of moping in my rooms and working out my own little methods of thought, so that I never mixed much with the men of my year. Bar fencing and boxing I had few athletic tastes and then my line of study was quite distinct from that of the other fellows, so that we had no points of contact at all."

Even the friendship with Trevor had an involuntary beginning. "Trevor was the only man I knew, and that only through the accident of his bull terrier freezing onto my ankle one morning as I went down to chapel. He was a hearty, full-blooded fellow, full of spirit and energy, the very opposite to me in most respects but we had some subjects in common, and it was a bond of union when I found that he was as friendless as I."

In fact, it was Trevor's father who intuitively spotted the likely future application of Holmes's remarkable skills. "It seems to me that all the detectives of fact and fancy would be children in your hands. That's your line of life, sir, and you may take the word of a man who has seen something of the world."

Holmes himself was coming to a similar conclusion. "My turn that way (to the arts) is in my veins, and may have come with my grandmother, who was the sister of Vernet, the French artist. Art in the blood is liable to take the strangest of forms . . ." By which he meant that the "faculty of observation and . . . peculiar facility for deduction" was something both he and Mycroft had somehow inherited.

[Emile Jean Horace Vernet (1789–1863) was a highly regarded French painter. When a branch of the family settled in England they anglicized the name to 'Verner.' Upon Holmes's return in 1894 he is anxious for the widowed Watson to move back to Baker Street. "At his request I had sold my practice . . . A young doc-

Horace Vernet, the French painter who was Holmes's great-uncle.

tor named Verner had purchased my small Kensington practice, and given with astonishingly little demur the highest price that I ventured to ask—an incident which only explained itself some years later, when I found that Verner was a distant relation of Holmes, and that it was my friend who had really found the money."]

Holmes wasted no time . . .

"When I first came up to London (1878) I had rooms in Montague Street, just around the corner from the British Museum, and there I waited, filling in my too abundant leisure time by studying all those branches of science which might make me more efficient. Now and again cases came my way, principally through the introduction of old fellow-students, for during my last years at the university there was a good deal of talk there about myself and my methods . . ."

"Even when you knew me first"—he tells Watson in "The Musgrave Ritual"—"I had already established a considerable, though not a very lucrative connection. You can hardly realise, then, how difficult I found it at first, and how long I had to wait before I succeeded in making any headway."

In those three years, however, he had laid the groundwork for the triumphs to come and his eventual position of "unofficial adviser and helper to everybody who is absolutely puzzled, throughout three continents." ("A Case of Identity")

* * * *

The man Watson met that day at St. Bart's cut an impressive figure . . .

"His very person and appearance were such as to strike the attention of the most casual observer. In height he was rather over six feet, and so excessively lean that he seemed to be considerably taller. His eyes were sharp and piercing . . . and his thin, hawk-like nose gave his whole expression an air of alertness and decision. His chin . . . had the prominence and squareness which mark the man of determination . . . His hands . . . possessed an extraordinary delicacy of touch." (*A Study in Scarlet*)

There were to be occasions when his height would prove a temporary disadvantage. In one of his many disguises he would often pass for someone much smaller and "It is no joke when a tall man has to take a foot off his height for an hour or more."

Over the years Watson is continually struck by that "tall, spare figure," sometimes that "tall gaunt figure," the "long thin form curled up in the recesses of his arm-chair," usually withdrawn and silent . . .

"He has been seated for some hours in silence, with his long, thin back curved over a chemical vessel in which he was brewing a particularly malodorous product. His head was sunk upon his breast, and he looked from my point of view like a strange, lank bird, with dull grey plumage and a black top-knot." ("The Dancing Men")

The bird imagery returns. Under "his bushy eyebrows" . . . "his beady eyes" were "gleaming and deep-set like those of a bird." Those eyes were gray and, when Holmes's attention was engaged, "as bright and keen as rapiers" or "shining like stars," transfixing the object of their attention "with their searching glance."

Equally, when that interest was withdrawn, it was as though a light switch had been thrown . . .

"He sat in his big arm-chair, with the weary heavy-lidded expression which veiled his keen and eager nature" or he would be found "staring up at the ceiling with dreamy, lack-lustre eyes," . . . "the introspective and pallid dreamer of Baker Street."

One person who found Holmes particularly impressive from the purely physiological point of view was Dr. Mortimer. When he comes to consult Holmes at the opening of *The Hound of the Baskervilles*, he can't take his eyes off the detective's head . . .

"I had hardly expected so dolichocephalic a skull or such well-marked supra-orbital development . . . A cast of your skull, sir, until the original is available, would be an ornament to any anthropological museum . . . I confess that I covet your skull."

[Professor Moriarty appears to have been less impressed. At their first meeting in "The Final Problem," "he peered . . . with great curiosity in his puckered eyes. 'You have less frontal development than I should have expected.' "]

Like the rest of his clients, Mortimer then found himself on the receiving end of Holmes's professional scrutiny, as he first gave "one of his quick, all comprehensive glances," and then "looked with the minute and yet abstracted fashion that was peculiar to him . . . and then composed himself with his lids drooping and his fingertips together to listen to (the) story."

Off duty Holmes was given to marked mood swings. "Holmes was in a mood which his friends would call taciturn, and others morose. He ran out and ran in, smoked incessantly, played snatches on his violin, sank into reveries, devoured sandwiches at irregular hours and hardly answered the casual questions I put to him." ("The Second Stain")

There was the introspective Holmes . . .

"He continued to walk up and down the room with his head sunk on his chest and his brows drawn down . . . and his hands clasped behind him . . . as was his habit when lost in thought." (A *Study in Scarlet*)

Often he would seek the solace of the "big arm-chair" . . . "He threw himself down onto the chair opposite and drew up his knees until his fingers clasped round his long, thin shins" or he "stuck his feet up on the corner of the mantelpiece and leaned back with his hands in his pockets." Sometimes the long thin legs would be stretched out towards the fire, while "he closed his eyes and showed not so much as the tremor of a lid." . . . "that Red Indian composure

"His eyes were bent over the glow of the fire." (Sidney Paget for "The Five Orange Pips," 1891)

which had made so many regard him as a machine rather than a man" ("The Crooked Man") . . . "He sat with the weary, heavy-lidded expression which concealed his keen and eager nature." ("The Engineer's Thumb")

Then there was the playful Holmes . . .

"He wriggled in his chair, as was his habit when in high spirits". . . "It seemed to me that he was making desperate efforts to restrain a convulsive attack of laughter . . . his whole body gave a wriggle of suppressed excitement.""Sometimes he was making progress and whistled and sang at his work." ("The Dancing Men")

One does not naturally associate Holmes with levity, yet he was easily amused by life's little ironies and his reaction ranged from "the sardonic smile which occasionally broke through his ascetic gloom" to the "silent laughter". . . "in the hearty, noiseless fashion that was peculiar to him." They were, however, "rare fits of laughter"—as Watson notes in *The Hound of the Baskervilles*—"I have not heard him laugh often, and it has always boded ill to somebody."

On occasion it was Watson who found himself the recipient. "His mood was particularly bright and joyous, with that somewhat sinister cheerfulness which was characteristic of his lighter moments.

'You have a case, Holmes?' I remarked.

'The faculty of deduction is certainly contagious, Watson. It has enabled you to probe my secret. Yes, I have a case . . .'" ("Thor Bridge")

*   *   *   *

Companion to the arm-chair was invariably a pipe and the habit Holmes warned Watson about at their first meeting. ("You don't mind the smell of strong tobacco, I hope?") He had almost certainly detected that Watson was a pipe smoker himself and that he was an Arcadia mixture man.

He kept a "litter of pipes" on the bedroom mantlepiece and his favorites in a pipe-rack. There was the "old and oily (black) clay pipe which was to him as a counsellor," which would have "thick blue cloud-wreaths spinning up" from it. "The unsavoury pipe which was the companion of his deepest meditations." (*The Valley of Fear*) Then there was "the long cherrywood which was wont to replace his clay" when he was "in a disputatious rather than a meditative mood."

These were his favorites by far and although most depictions of Holmes insist on showing him with a hooked pipe, "his great yellowed meerschaum" was, in reality, not his boon companion when he "retired to his chair to brood, long legs outstretched, chin on chest . . . brows knotted . . . billows of smoke rising . . . from the reeking amber of his pipe." A pipe with an amber stem and a briar completed his rack of favorites.

It was his habit to smoke one pipe before breakfast, made up of "all the plugs and dottles left from his smokes of the day before, all carefully dried and collected on the corner of the mantlepiece." After breakfast he would have another, presumably using a fresh supply of the strong black tobacco, thus starting the supply chain that would lead to the next day.

His favorite tobacco was "Bradley's strongest shag . . . the acrid fumes of strongest, coarse tobacco which took me by the throat and set me coughing."

The pipe appears to have been his principal aid to concentrated thought . . . ("Holmes leaned back . . . and blew little wavering rings of smoke up to the ceiling . . . put his finger tips together and assumed his most impassive and judicial expression"). A particularly knotty problem was one he would describe as "quite a three pipe problem and I beg that you won't speak to me for fifty minutes." ("The Red-Headed League") In the case of "The Man with the Twisted Lip" Holmes sat up all night smoking, until he had solved the

"The pipe was still between his lips." (Sidney Paget for "The Man with the
Twisted Lip," 1891)

problem—"by sitting upon five pillows and consuming an ounce of shag." At which point he no doubt "sat up . . . and took his pipe out of his mouth, like a hound that has heard the 'View Halloo."

Nonetheless, Holmes was addicted to all forms of tobacco. He would frequently celebrate a success with "a whisky and soda and cigar"—presumably extracted from the toe of the Persian slipper, although there is evidence that he carried a supply. On one occasion he would be ready to leave Baker Street, "when I have changed my dressing-gown and filled my cigar case." Nor, in a more casual moment, was he even averse to a cigarette—"He sent up a great blue triumphant cloud from his cigarette." ("A Scandal in Bohemia") "He lit a cigarette in his old nonchalant manner." ("The Empty House")

Presumably he also took snuff occasionally or why else would the King of Bohemia present him with a valuable snuff box? ("Take a pinch of snuff, Doctor, and acknowledge that I have scored over you.") ("A Case of Identity")

"For goodness' sake, let us have a quiet pipe and turn our minds for a few hours to something more cheerful." ("The Speckled Band")

* * * *

Once Holmes was on the scent, an entirely different body language took over. Gone was the gaunt figure in the arm-chair, "biting his nails" in frustration because he had no case to divert him. Instead . . .

"His face flushed and darkened, his brows were drawn into two hard, black lines, while his eyes shone out from beneath them with a steely glitter. His face was bent forward, his shoulders bowed, his lips compressed, and the veins stood out like whipcord in his long, sinewy neck. His nostrils seemed to dilate with a purely animal lust for the chase and his mind was so absolutely concentrated upon the matter

"For a long time he remained there." (Sidney Paget for "The Boscombe Valley Mystery," 1891)

before him, that a question or remark fell unheeded upon his ears, or at the most only provoked a quick, impatient snarl in reply." ("The Boscombe Valley Mystery")

"As I watched him I was irresistibly reminded of a pure-blooded, well-trained foxhound, as it dashes backward and forward through the covert, whining in its eagerness, until it comes across the lost scent." (*A Study in Scarlet*)

"His eager, questioning eyes were fixed, and I saw on his keen, alert face that tightening of the lips, that quiver of the nostrils, and concentration of the heavy tufted brows which I knew so well . . . that expression of intense and high-strung energy." ("The Bruce-Partington Plans")

"His pale, eager face had suddenly assumed that tense far-away expression which I had learned to associate with the supreme manifestations of his genius." ("Thor Bridge")

"His chin upon his chest and his brows knitted, charging and recharging his pipe with the strongest black tobacco . . . his sharp, eager face framed in his ear-flapped travelling cap." ("Silver Blaze")

"His eyes were shining and his cheeks tinged with colour. Only at a crisis have I seen those battle-signals flying." ("The Golden Pince-Nez")

And woe betide the object of such scrutiny—in this case Baron Gruner . . .

"Holmes's eyes . . . contracted and lightened until they were like two menacing points of steel . . . 'You are absolutely plate-glass. I see to the very back of your mind.'" ("The Illustrious Client")

"So swift, silent and furtive were his movements, like those of a trained bloodhound picking out a scent, that I could not but think what a terrible criminal he would have made had he turned his energy and sagacity against the law instead of exerting them in its defence." (*The Sign of Four*)

The *dénouement*, of course, was often preceded by a certain amount of physical activity which distinctly deterred brother Mycroft from pursuing Holmes's chosen profession . . . "to run here and there, to cross-question railway guards, and lie on my face with a lens to my eye—it is not my *métier*." ("The Bruce-Partington Plans") "He threw himself down upon his face with his lens in his hand, and crawled swiftly backwards and forwards, examining minutely . . ."

* * * *

Again and again, Watson stresses the duality of Holmes's nature, the medico-turned-psychiatrist . . .

"In his singular character the dual nature alternately asserted itself, and his extreme exactness and astuteness represented, as I have often thought, the reaction to the poetic and contemplative mood which occasionally predominated in him. The swing of his nature took him from extreme langour to devouring energy . . . He was never so truly formidable as when, for days on end, he had been lounging in his arm-chair amid his (violin) improvisation and his black-letter editions. Then it was that the lust of the chase would suddenly come upon him . . . " ("The Red-Headed League")

"What are my other shortcomings?" Holmes asks himself rhetorically, when he and Watson first meet. "I get in the dumps at times, and don't open my mouth for days on end. You must not think I am sulky when I do that. Just let me alone and I'll soon be all right . . . "

He was perfectly capable of analyzing himself as if he had been his own client . . .

"I have a curious constitution. I never remember feeling tired by work, though idleness exhausts me completely. My mind rebels at stagnation. Give me problems, give me work, give me the most abstruse cryptogram, or the most intricate analysis, and I am in my

"All afternoon he sat in the stall (at St. James's Hall)." (Sidney Paget for "The Red-Headed League," 1891)

own proper atmosphere. I can dispense then with artificial stimulants. But I abhor the dull routine of existence. I crave for mental exaltation." (*The Sign of Four*)

Watson learned to recognize the signs of preoccupation . . .

"It is when he is on the scent and is not quite absolutely sure yet that it is the right one that he is most taciturn." ("The Naval Treaty")

"When he had an unsolved problem upon his mind, he would go for days, even for a week, without rest, turning it over, rearranging his facts, looking at it from every point of view, until he had either fathomed it or convinced himself that his data were insufficient." ("The Man with the Twisted Lip")

"It was one of Holmes's characteristics that he could command sleep at will. Unfortunately he could resist it at will also, and often have I had to remonstrate with him on the harm he must be doing himself when, deeply engrossed in one of his strange or baffling problems, he would go for several consecutive days and nights without one wink of sleep. He put the shades over the lamps, lent back in his corner, and in less than two minutes his regular breathing told me he was fast asleep. Not being blessed with the same gift myself, I lay back in my corner for some time nodding to the rhythmical throb of the express as it hurled itself forward through the darkness. Now and again as we shot through some brilliantly illuminated station or past a line of flaming furnaces, I caught for an instant a glimpse of Holmes's figure coiled up snugly in the far corner with his head sunk upon his breast."

In this mood he was oblivious to anything and anyone outside his narrow focus.

"Without having a tinge of cruelty in his singular composition, he was undoubtedly callous from long over-stimulation. Yet, if his emotions were dulled, his intellectual perceptions were exceedingly alive . . . his face showed the rather quiet and interested composure of the chemist who sees the crystals falling into position from his over-saturated solution." (The Valley of Fear)

It was fortunate for Holmes that he had a roommate who was technically as well as temperamentally qualified to understand him. And, every now and then, even Watson felt he had reached the boundary . . .

"You would certainly have been burned had you lived a few centuries ago." ("A Scandal in Bohemia")

*   *   *   *

That dead zone between cases was the ennui Holmes feared all his professional life. "Alas, I already feel it closing in upon me! My life is spent in one long effort to escape from the commonplace existence" ("The Red-Headed League") It was what led him—in the early years of his relationship with Watson—to indulge in taking drugs—a habit which at the time, was perfectly legal. His addiction was to both morphine and cocaine ("Which is it today?" Watson asks him), the infamous "seven per cent solution," the drug and the syringe being housed in a "neat morocco case." "I suppose that its influence is physically a bad one. I find it, however, so transcendentally stimulating and clarifying to the mind that its secondary action is a matter of small moment." (The Sign of Four)

His dependency preceded Watson, who observed in A Study in Scarlet that "for days on end (Holmes) would lie upon the sofa in the sitting-room, hardly uttering a word or moving a muscle from morning to night. On these occasions I have noticed such a dreamy vacant expression in his eyes, that I might have suspected him of being addicted to the use of some narcotic, had not the temperament of his whole life forbidden such a notion."

"Holmes was working hard over a chemical investigation." (Sidney Paget
for "The Naval Treaty," 1893)

It does not take a trained medical man long to confirm his suspicions that his friend is a "self-poisoner," and the shadow of the drug is one they both have to learn to live with in those early years. By the time of "A Scandal in Bohemia" (1888) Watson was recording that Holmes would remain in Baker Street. "Buried among his old books, and alternating week to week between cocaine and ambition, the drowsiness of the drug, and the fierce energy of his own keen nature . . . his drug-created dreams."

Before the Reichenbach affair in 1891—Watson would write later—"For years I had gradually weaned him from that drug mania which had threatened once to check his remarkable career. Now I knew that under ordinary conditions he no longer craved for this artificial stimulus, but I was well aware that the fiend was not dead but sleeping, and I have known that the sleep was a light one and the waking near when in periods of idleness I have seen the drawn look upon Holmes's ascetic face, and the brooding of his deep-set and inscrutable eyes." ("The Missing Three-Quarter")

By 1896 Watson felt the habit was at least under control.

* * * *

At college Holmes laid claim to "few athletic tastes . . . bar fencing and boxing" and in the case of "The Missing Three-Quarter" he observes sardonically and self-respectively that "My ramifications stretch out into many sections of society, but never . . . into amateur sport, which is the best and soundest thing in England."

Nonetheless—perhaps in the privacy of his own room, since we are never witness to it—he made a point of keeping himself in good physical shape. Even Watson declared himself surprised, since his friend was "a man who seldom took exercise for exercise's sake. Few men were capable of greater muscular effort . . . "—as when he unbent the poker that Grimesby Roylott had previously bent for effect in "The Speckled Band"—"and he was undoubtedly one of the finest boxers of his weight that I have ever seen; but he looked upon aimless bodily exertion as a waste of energy and he seldom bestirred himself save where there was some professional object to be served. That he should have kept himself in training under such circumstances is remarkable but his diet was usually of the sparest and his habits were simple to the verge of austerity." ("The Yellow Face")

Although Watson does not record it in detail, it is obvious that Holmes kept up his interest in boxing and took part in at least one 'benefit' as an amateur at Alison's Rooms, where he fought three rounds with the recipient, the professional McMurdo. When the two meet again in *The Sign of Four* McMurdo recalls their encounter "four years back" (1884?). "God's truth! . . . If instead o' standing there so quiet you had just stepped in and given me that cross-hit of yours under the jaw, I'd ha' known you without a question . . . You might have aimed high, if you had joined the fancy."

"You are aware that I have some proficiency in the good old British sport of boxing. Occasionally it is of service . . ." ("The Solitary Cyclist")

Although Holmes was caused to defend himself with his fists on more than one occasion, he was inclined to take other precautions. "The loaded hunting-crop was his favourite weapon," Watson noted and Holmes himself reminded him in "The Illustrious Client" that "I'm a bit of a single-stick expert, as you know."

But perhaps the skill which was to prove most useful was the most arcane for an Englishman of the period. Explaining to Watson in "The Empty House" how he came to save himself from the clutches of Professor Moriarty on the Reichenbach Falls, he says modestly—"I have some knowledge of baritsu, the

Japanese system of wrestling, which has more than once been very useful to me."

One game that one would have expected to fit that precise mind to a 't' is chess—yet we never see Holmes playing chess and the references to it are oblique and contradictory.

In "The Mazarin Stone" Holmes looks at his opponent, Count Silvius "thoughtfully, like a master chess-player who meditates his crowning move." Yet in "The Retired Colourman" he warns Watson—"(He) excelled at chess—one mark, Watson, of a scheming mind."

*   *   *   *

"And I return with an excellent appetite." ("Black Peter")

"He walked up to the sideboard, and tearing a piece from the loaf he devoured it voraciously, washing it down with a long draught of water.'You are hungry!' I remarked." ("The Five Orange Pips")

Holmes as gourmet? At first glance the idea seems absurd. The image we have of him is of an ascetic who uses food only as fuel, but the image is misleading.

When involved in a case, he could and did go without food for days at a time. "It was one of his peculiarities that in his more intense moments he would permit himself no food, and I have known him presume on his iron strength until he has fainted from pure inanition.'At present I cannot spare energy and nerve force for digestion,' he would say in answer to my medical remonstrances." ("The Noble Bachelor") And in "The Mazarin Stone" (1903) Billy, the page, would report to Watson—who hardly needed to be told—that when his master was on a case, "he gets paler and thinner and he eats nothing."

But these were the exceptions. On a good day Holmes believed in a hearty breakfast as a start to the day. "In the morning

I was up betimes, but some toast crumbs and two empty egg-shells told me that my companion was earlier still." First things came first. "When I have exterminated that fourth egg I will be ready to put you in touch with the whole situation." (*The Valley of Fear*) And when Watson brings back Victor Hatherley, the unfortunate engineer in "The Engineer's Thumb," Holmes "ordered fresh rashers and eggs and joined us in a hearty meal." . . . "Holmes swallowed a cup of coffee and turned his attention to the ham and eggs." ("The Naval Treaty")

In the same story, Holmes makes his remark about Mrs. Hudson's cuisine being "a little limited" but exempts her "excellent" breakfasts. "Uncovering a dish of curried chicken," he admits that she has "risen to the occasion."

Nor was his taste limited to good plain cooking. When dinner was served in Baker Street, it seems likely that Holmes supervised the preparation himself. "Watson, you have never yet recognised my abilities as a housekeeper," he teases his friend in *The Sign of Four*, when he invites Inspector Athelney Jones to join them. "I have oysters and a brace of grouse, with something a little choice in white wines." A good port is served after the meal and, since Jones is to stay in Baker Street overnight to make an early start the next day, the domestic Holmes briefly emerges. "I'll light my spirit-lamp and give you a cup of coffee before we start."

Holmes seemed rather partial to game. He once mentioned his predisposition to "dine at seven" and on that occasion "woodcock" was on the menu. In "The Noble Bachelor" he served "a couple of brace of cold woodcock, a pheasant, a *pâté de foie gras* pie with a group of ancient and cobwebby bottles." (Another proof of his using Mrs. Hudson's cellar?) "There is a cold partridge on the sideboard and a bottle of Montrachet. Let us renew our energies before we make a fresh call on them." ("The Bruce-Partington Plans")

When food was on his mind, Holmes did not like to miss a meal and preferred to dine at 7:00 P.M. ("Black Peter"). "We have two hours before we need to think of starting. I think we might employ it in getting some dinner." (*The Hound of the Baskervilles*) . . . "We shall have time for a mouthful of dinner before we need go." ("The Empty House") . . .

"Drive us to some decent hotel where we may have some lunch." ("The Cardboard Box") . . . "The question now is whether we should take a premature lunch here, or run our chance of starving before we reach the buffet at Newhaven." ("The Final Problem") "I never needed it more," said Holmes as he refreshed himself with a glass of claret and some biscuits . . . "However, as you know, my habits are irregular." . . . "I think something nutritious at Simpson's would not be out of place." ("The Dying Detective") "We can stop at Marcini's for a little dinner on the way." (*The Hound of the Baskervilles*) . . . "By Jove! My dear fellow, it is nearly nine, and the landlady babbled of green peas at seven-thirty. What with your eternal tobacco Watson, and your irregularity at meals, I expect that you will get notice to quit, and that I shall share your downfall." ("The Three Students")

"And now, if we are too late for dinner, I think we are both ready for our suppers." (*The Hound of the Baskervilles*) For one particular supper in Baker Street they sit down to the goose they had just been investigating. ("The Blue Carbuncle")

When eating out Holmes was known to have frequented Goldini's in the Gloucester Road, ("garish Italian") ("Join me in a coffee and curacao. Try one of the proprietor's cigars. They are less poisonous than one would expect."—"The Bruce-Partington Plans"), Marcini's and the Café Royal, but one has a distinct impression that, when a celebration was called for, his favorite watering hole was undoubtedly the 'nutritious' Simpson's-in-the-Strand.

* * * *

A celebratory—or even simply a relaxing—evening would invariably include music . . .

"Let us escape from this weary workaday world by the side door of music. Carina sings tonight at the Albert Hall, and we still have time to dress . . ." ("Shoscombe Old Place") . . . "a Joachim recital at the St. James's Hall" . . . "I have a box for *Les Huguenots*. Have you heard the De Reskes?" (brothers Jean and Edouard) (*The Hound of the Baskervilles*) . . . "the Hallé to hear (Wilma) Norman-Neruda" . . . "Her attack and her bowing are splendid. What's the little thing of Chopin's she plays so magnificently : Tra-la-la-lira-lira-lay" (*A Study in Scarlet*) . . . "a Wagner night at Covent Garden" ("The Retired Colourman")

"Do you remember what Darwin says about music? He claims that the power of producing and appreciating it existed among the human race long before the power of speech was arrived at. Perhaps that is why we are so subtly influenced by it. There are vague memories in our souls of those misty centuries when the world was in its childhood." (*A Study in Scarlet*)

Listening to Sarasate at the St. James's Hall . . . "All the afternoon he sat in the stalls wrapped in the most perfect happiness, gently waving his long, thin fingers in time to the music, while his gently smiling face and his languid, dreamy eyes were as unlike those of Holmes, the sleuth-hound, Holmes the relentless, keen-witted, ready-handed criminal agent, as it was possible to conceive." ("The Red Headed League")

[Pablo de Sarasate (1844–1908) was a Spanish violinist and composer.]

"Violin land, where all is sweetness, and delicacy, and harmony . . ."

Holmes himself—according to Watson—"was an enthusiastic musician, being himself not only a very capable performer but a composer of no ordinary merit." His instrument of choice was the violin and he was inordinately proud of the Stradivarius he had purchased from "a Jew broker" in the Tottenham Court Road for fifty-five shillings, which he claimed to be worth at least five hundred guineas. "Do you consider violin playing in your category of row?" he asked Watson when they are discussing sharing rooms.

His knowledge of violins was extensive. In *A Study in Scarlet* he "was in the best of spirits, and prattled away about Cremona fiddles, and the difference between a Stradivarius and an Amati."

"Draw your chair up and hand me my violin, for the only problem which we still have to solve is how to while away these bleak autumnal evenings." ("The Noble Bachelor") And, indeed, Holmes's "favourite occupation of scraping upon his violin" ("My fiddle would be the better for new strings.") was to become an integral part of their life together.

If Watson was not in the mood, then it seemed that "long into the stretches of the night I heard the low, melancholy wailings of his violin." (*A Study in Scarlet*). On a good day, however, he found almost as much pleasure in his friend's playing as Holmes himself . . .

"He began to play some low, dreamy, melodious air—his own, no doubt, for he had a remarkable gift for improvisation."

"His powers . . . were remarkable, but as eccentric as all his other accomplishments . . . he could play difficult pieces (like Mendelssohn's *lieder*) . . . When left to himself . . . he would seldom produce any music or attempt any recognised air. Leaning back in his arm-chair of an evening, he would close his eyes and scrape carelessly at the fiddle which was thrown across his knee. Sometimes the chords were sonorous and melancholy. Occasionally they were fantastic and cheerful. Clearly they reflected the thoughts which possessed him, but whether the music aided those thoughts, or whether the playing was simply the result of a whim or fancy was more than I could determine."

"I might have rebelled against these exasperating solos had it not been that he usually terminated them by playing in quick succession a whole series of my favourite airs as a slight compensation for the trial upon my patience." (A *Study in Scarlet*)

On one occasion at least Holmes's playing must have been superlative. To distract the villains in "The Mazarin Stone" Holmes pretends to go into his bedroom to play the Hoffmann Barcarolle, though in reality he switches places with a lifelike wax dummy, so as to overhear their confession—the identical trick he had played in "The Empty House." When they are duly amazed that he can be in two places at once—"These modern gramophones are a remarkable invention," Holmes calmly remarks.

Since the piece had to cover several minutes of conversation and was still playing when he unmasked them, it must have been a twelve-inch record. Even more remarkable, it must have been an unaccompanied violin and since there are no such records in existence then or now, it must have been specially cut by Holmes himself. [Should it, by any chance, still exist, it would undoubtedly fetch an incredible price at Sotheby's or Christie's today.]

When the musical mood took him, "he would talk about nothing but violins . . . This led him to Paganini, and we sat for an hour over a bottle of claret while he told me anecdote after anecdote of that extraordinary man." ("The Cardboard Box.")

[Niccolo Paganini (1782–1840) was a great Italian violinist.]

Apart from his devotion to both the opera and the concert hall, Holmes had a keen interest in medieval English music and the motets of the Flemish composer, Orlandus Lassus (1532–1594). In "The Bruce-Partington Plans" Watson records that he had written a monograph on "The Polyphonic Motets of Lassus" (1898) . . . "which he has since printed for private circulation, and is said by experts to be the last word on the subject." In general he preferred the German composers, such as Wagner, Haydn, and Mendelssohn to the French and Italian. "It is introspective, and I want to introspect. Come along!" ("The Red-Headed League")

* * * *

When it came to the monograph, Holmes was quite a prolific author—("I have been guilty of several monographs. They are all upon technical subjects.") Soon after they moved into Baker Street Watson was leafing through a magazine left on the table and came across an article entitled *The Book of Life* (1881), which "attempted to show how much an observant man might learn by an accurate and systematic examination of all that came in his way." He is loudly skeptical of its author's claims—until he learns that Holmes wrote the piece.

In *The Sign of Four* Holmes reveals that he has also published monographs on tobacco . . . *Upon the Distinction between the Ashes of the Various Tobaccos* on *Ennumeration of 140 Forms of Cigar, Cigarette and Pipe Tobacco with Coloured Plates Illustrating the Difference in the Ash* (1879) . . . "It is a point which is continually turning up in criminal trials, and which is sometimes of supreme importance as a clue." . . . "To the trained eye there is as much difference between the black ash of a Trichinopoly and the white fluff of bird's eye as there is between a cabbage and a potato." ("The Boscombe Valley Mystery") Since the "coloured plates" were certainly illustrations, can we add 'drawing' to the catalogue of Holmes's artistic skills?

The Tracing of Footsteps (with Some Remarks upon the Uses of Plaster of Paris as a Preserver of Impresses)

. . . "The Influence of a Trade upon the Form of a Hand, with lithotypes of the hands of slaters, sailors, cork-cutters, compositors, weavers, and diamond-polishers. That is a matter of great practical interest to the scientific detective—especially in cases of unclaimed bodies, or in discovering the antecedents of criminals.". . . "There is no part of the body which varies as much as the human ear. Each ear is as a rule quite distinctive, and differs from all other ones. In last year's *Anthropological Journal* you will find two short monographs from my pen upon the subject." (*On Variations in the Human Ear*, 1886)

In other monographs he had analyzed *The Uses of Dogs in Detecting* . . . ("My line of thought about dogs is analogous. A dog reflects the family life. And their passing moods may reflect the passing moods of others." ("The Creeping Man") Holmes seems to have had a distinctly soft spot for dogs in general and referred to their "beautiful, faithful nature" in "The Lion's Mane."

(Incidentally, whatever happened to the "bull pup" Watson claimed to have when he and Holmes first met?)

"Then there were the one hundred and sixty separate ciphers." *(On Secret Writings)* ("There are many ciphers which I would read as easily as I do the apochrypha of the agony column. Such crude devices amuse the intelligence without fatiguing it.") . . . "I have made a small study of tattoo marks *(On Tattoo Marks)* and have even contributed to the literature of the subject.". . . "a typewriter has really quite as much individuality as a man's handwriting . . . I think of writing another little monograph some of these days *On the Typewriter and its Relation to Crime.* It is a subject to which I have devoted some little attention". . . "malingering is a subject upon which I have sometimes thought of writing a monograph" . . . and one *On the Dating of Documents* . . .

Elsewhere in an odd moment we come across Holmes conducting "laborious researches into *Early English Charters,* researches which led to results so striking that they may be the subject of one of my future narratives"; manuscripts . . . and on another occasion "He was engaged with a powerful lens deciphering the remains of the original inscription upon a palimpsest" . . . in Cornwall the study of

Chaldean Roots in the Ancient Cornish Language ("The ancient Cornish language had arrested his attention and he had . . . conceived the idea that it was akin to the Chaldean (Aramaic) and had been largely derived from the Phoenician traders in tin.)"

And, of course, he always intended to devote much of his retirement to writing ("I propose to devote my declining years to the composition of a textbook which shall focus *The Whole Art of Detection* into one volume."—"The Abbey Grange") It is doubtful if he ever brought himself to complete it—since Watson was to report his time was "divided between philosophy and agriculture—but he most certainly did produce his *chef d'oeuvre*—the *Practical Handbook of Bee Culture with Some Observations upon the Segregation of the Queen.*" When he meets Watson for the last recorded time in "His Last Bow," he tells him of "the fruit of my leisured ease, the magnum opus of my latter years . . . Alone I did it. Behold the fruit of pensive nights laborious days, when I watched the little working groups as once I watched the criminal world of London."

* * * *

Soon after they move into 221B Watson finds himself intrigued by the range of Holmes's knowledge ("He did not appear to have pursued any course of reading which might fit him for a degree in science or any other recognised portal which would give him an entrance into the learned world, yet . . . within eccentric limits his knowledge was so extraordinarily ample and minute") and appalled at what he considers to be the gaps in it. One day he decides to make a list in pencil. "I could not help smiling at the document when I had completed it." Indeed, he must have shaken his head ruefully over the memory of it many a time in the years ahead, as Holmes continually revealed new depths.

SHERLOCK HOLMES—HIS LIMITS

1. Knowledge of Literature — Nil
2. Knowledge of Philosophy — Nil
3. Knowledge of Astronomy — Nil
4. Knowledge of Politics — Feeble
5. Knowledge of Botany — Variable. Well up in belladonna, opium, and poisons generally. Knows nothing of practical gardening.
6. Knowledge of Geology — Practical, but limited. Tells at a glance different soils from each other. After walks has shown me splashes upon his trousers and told me by their color and consistence in what part of London he had received them.
7. Knowledge of Chemistry — Profound
8. Knowledge of Anatomy — Accurate, but unsystematic
9. Knowledge of Sensational Literature — Immense. He appears to know every detail of every horror perpetrated in the century.
10. Plays the violin well.
11. Is an expert singlestick player, boxer, and swordsman.
12. He has a good practical knowledge of British law.

"When I had got so far in my list I threw it into the fire in despair." Naturally, a man with Holmes's questing mind was always adding to his store of knowledge and he would certainly have filled in numerous gaps in his knowledge as the years went by, but it is hard to resist the conclusion that Holmes sensed from the very first that Watson could be made to rise to the bait and was inclined to indulge his sardonic humor at his friend's expense. There is obvious irony—even though Watson seems unaware of it—in A *Study in Scarlet* . . .

"His ignorance was as remarkable as his knowledge. Of contemporary literature, philosophy and politics he appeared to know next to nothing . . ." When Watson quoted Thomas Carlyle (1795–1881), the famous historian and essayist, Holmes "inquired in the naivest way who he might be and what he had done." Yet not long afterwards Holmes is paraphrasing one of Carlyle's best known *dicta* as "They say that genius is an infinite capacity for taking pains." (What Carlyle had actually written was—"Genius . . . which is the transcendent capacity for taking trouble first of all"—*Life of Frederick the Great*)

Watson was equally appalled that Holmes appeared ignorant of the Copernican Theory of the universe and the composition of the Solar System ("That any civilised human being of the nineteenth century should not be aware that the earth travelled round the sun . . .") To which Holmes replied—"You say that we go round the sun. If we went round the moon it would not make a pennyworth of difference to me or my work . . . Now that I do know it, I shall do my best to forget it . . . " He then proceeds to give Watson a little lesson in the philosophy of Sherlock Holmes—"I consider that a man's brain originally is like a little empty attic, and you have to stock it with such furniture as you choose. A fool takes in all the lumber of every sort he comes across, so that the knowledge which might be useful to him gets crowded out or at best is jumbled up with a lot of other things, so that he has a difficulty in laying his hands upon it. Now the skilled workman is very careful indeed as to what he takes into his brain-attic. He will have nothing but the tools which may help him in doing his work, but of these he has a large assortment, and all in the most perfect order. It is a mistake to think that that little room has elastic walls and can distend to any extent. Depend upon it, there comes a time when for every addition of knowledge you forget something you knew before. It is of the highest importance, therefore, not to have useless facts elbowing out the useful ones."

In "The Five Orange Pips" he would extend the image a little by suggesting that "the rest he can put away in the lumber-room of his library, where he can get it if he wants it," though late in his career—in "The Lion's Mane"—he would modify that view slightly, saying that his own mind was "like a crowded box-room with packets of all sorts stowed away therein—so many that I may well have but a vague perception of what was there." But that, perhaps, was a symptom that even Sherlock Holmes was not impervious to the aging process.

Nonetheless, Holmes found space in his "little attic" for an eclectic range of material . . .

"Education never ends, Watson. It is a series of lessons with the greatest for the last." ("The Red Circle")

"He spoke on a quick succession of subjects—on miracle plays, on medieval pottery, on Stradivarius violins, on the Buddhism of Ceylon and on the warships of the future—handling each as though he had made a special study of it." (*The Sign of Four*)

"Jean Paul Richter . . . makes one curious but profound remark. It is that the chief proof of man's real greatness lies in his perception of his own smallness. There is much food for thought in Richter." (*The Sign of Four*)

[Richter (1763–1825) was a Swiss-German writer, mainly of romances and essays.]

Despite Watson's early verdict of "Literature—Nil," Holmes could claim—"I am an omnivorous reader" ("The Lion's Mane") and even though that was late in his career, the evidence was always in his favor . . .

"Let me recommend this book—one of the most remarkable ever penned. It is Winwood Reade's *Martyrdom of Man*—a defence of scientific agnosticism." ("He remarks that, while the individual man is an insoluble puzzle, in the aggregate he becomes a mathematical certainty.") (*The Sign of Four*) . . . "You should read De Quincey's *On Murder Considered As One of the Fine Arts* (1827) . . ." "when an artist turns to murder, it augurs well for the student of unusual psychiatric syndromes." . . . "Circumstantial evidence is occasionally very convincing, as when you find a trout in the milk, to quote Thoreau's example." . . . "You may remember the old Persian saying, 'There is danger for him who taketh the tiger cub, and danger also for whoso snatches a delusion from a woman.' There is as much sense in Hafiz as in Horace, as much knowledge of the world." ("A Case of Identity")

[Hafiz was a Persian lyric poet of the fourteenth century whose work was first published in England in 1891.]

"And now let us talk about George Meredith, if you please." ("The Boscombe Valley Mystery") [Meredith (1828–1909) seems have been Holmes's favorite contemporary novelist.] During the same adventure he carried around a "pocket Petrarch." [Francesco Petrarch (1304–1374), an Italian lyric poet] and in *A Study in Scarlet* he was reading "a queer old book I picked up at a stall yesterday—*De Jure inter Gentes (On the Law among Peoples)*—published in Latin at Liège in the Lowlands, in 1642."

He was known to quote Latin on several occasions. In "The Red-Headed League" it was from Tacitus:

Omne ignotum pro magnifico
("Everything unknown is considered something splendid")

Shakespeare was a regular standby. Holmes's famous line—first used in "The Abbey Grange"—"The game is afoot!" derives from *Henry V* . . .

> I see you stand like greyhounds in the slips,
> Straining upon the start. The game's afoot:
> Follow your spirit; and, upon this charge
> Cry "God for Harry! England and St. George!"

. . . and when he says that the landlady at their country hotel had "babbled of green peas at seven-thirty," he is, of course, parodying another line from the same play—when the Hostess of the inn tells how the dying Falstaff has "a babbled of green fields."

In "The Disappearance of Lady Frances Carfax" he quotes from *Henry VI* (Part II) (Act III.Sc.2).

> Thrice is he armed who hath his quarrel just

. . . and in "The Empty House" from *Antony and Cleopatra:*

> Age cannot wither her, nor custom stale her infinite variety.
> (Act II : Sc. 2)

"'I trust that age doth not wither nor custom stale my infinite variety,' said he . . ."

. . . comparing himself to that timeless courtesan . . .

. . . though in "The Empty House" he misquotes *Twelfth Night* . . .

"Journeys end in lovers' meetings"

. . . which should read . . .

Journeys end in lovers meeting

When—in "A Case of Identity"—he claims that "Life . . . would make all fiction . . . most stale and unprofitable," he is, of course, paraphrasing Hamlet:

How weary, stale, flat, and unprofitable
Seem to me all the uses of this world

. . . while his proud boast in telling Watson about his book on bee culture—Alone I Did It—is from *Coriolanus* (Act V).

"My Biblical knowledge is a trifle rusty, I fear," Holmes disclaims in "The Crooked Man," but he still recalls that "the small affair of Uriah and Bathsheba" will be found "in the first or second of Samuel," (in fact Samuel 11–13) and when (in *The Valley of Fear*) he talks to Watson about the need to "possess our souls in patience," he is paraphrasing Luke 21:19— "In your patience possess ye your souls."

At the end of "The Speckled Band" he reflects on the ironic fate that befalls Grimesby Roylott—"the schemer falls into the pit which he digs for another," a reference to "He that diggeth a pit shall fall into it." (Ecclesiastes 1:2)

. . . while in "The Illustrious Client" he invokes "the wages of sin" (Romans 6:23)

Nor was his literary ability to quote restricted to the English language . . .

"Wir sind gewohnt, dass die Menschen verhöhnen / Was sie nicht verstehen." ("We are accustomed to seeing man despite what he does not understand"—*Faust*, 1790) "*Goethe is always pithy.*" (*The Sign of Four*)

"Though unmusical, German is the most expressive of all languages" ("His Last Bow")

"Shade dass die Natur einen Mensch aus der schuf,/ Dem zum wurdigen Mann war und zum Schelmen der Stoff" ("It is a shame that Nature made only one person out of you, for there was material enough for a good man and a rogue.") (*Xenian*—1796)

In French he liked to quote the end line of Nicolas Despreaux's (1636–1711) *L'Art Poetique*—

Un sot trouve toujours un plus sot qui l'admire

("A fool can always find a greater fool to admire him")

Holmes also liked to quote Gustave Flaubert's remark in a letter to the writer, George Sand—*"L'homme n'est rien, l'oeuvre—tout"* (The man is nothing, work is everything.") He did, however, get it slightly wrong. The line should read—*"L'homme c'est rien—l'oeuvre c'est tout."*

"Voilà tout! . . . nous verrons."

There is evidence in the text that Holmes spoke (at least passably) French, German, Italian, Norwegian, Dutch, Arabic, Latin and at the very least and he had enough knowledge of other languages to be able to relate Cornish to Chaldean.

At the very end of his career he even attempted that most deceptive of languages—American English. "American slang is very expressive sometimes." ("The Noble Bachelor")

As the 'Irish-American' agent, Altamont in "His Last Bow" Holmes uses such expressions of would be American idiom as . . . "give me the glad hand" . . . "I'm bringing home the bacon" . . . "the dough" . . . "the boodle" . . . "stunt" . . . "It's enough to make a man bughouse" . . . "it would have been nitsky for you and me" . . . "I beg your pardon, Watson, my well of English seems to be permanently defiled."

*   *   *   *

Although he didn't mention it specifically in his list, Watson might easily have added "Art—Nil." In *The Hound of the Baskervilles* he is irritated that "For two hours the strange business in which he had been involved appeared to be forgotten and he was entirely absorbed in the pictures of the modern Belgian masters. He would talk of nothing but art, of which he had the crudest of ideas." Once again, one must question his judgment.

During the very same adventure Holmes shows considerable knowledge of portraiture when the two of them examine the gallery at Baskerville Hall:

"Watson won't allow that I know anything of art, but that is mere jealousy, because our views on the subject differ."

"A study of family portraits is enough to convert a man to the doctrine of reincarnation . . . I know what is good when I see it, and I see it now. That's a Kneller, I'll swear, that lady in the blue silk over yonder, and the stout gentleman with the wig ought to be a Reynolds."

[Sir Godfrey Kneller (1649–1723) was a British portrait painter and Sir Joshua Reynolds (1723–1792) an even greater one.]

He was also well informed about Moriarty's favorite artist, Jean-Baptiste Greuze (1725–1805), the Frenchman who specialized in moralistic and sentimental subjects . . . "Modern criticism has more than endorsed the high opinion formed of him by his contemporaries . . . in the year 1865 a picture entitled *La Jeune Fille a l'Agneau* fetched not less than four thousand pounds." (*The Valley of Fear*) Moriarty owned and greatly prized a Greuze showing "a young woman with her head on her hands, keaking at you sideways." (Possibly *Girl with Arms Folded*)

* * * *

Watson chose to regard both Holmes and himself as being of a 'Bohemian' disposition, because of their unconventional lifestyle but, in truth, only Holmes qualified. "He loathed every form of society with his whole Bohemian soul" and regarded any form of social invitation as one of "those unwelcome summonses which call upon a man either to be bored or to lie." ("The Noble Bachelor") A line which sounds more like Oscar Wilde than Sherlock Holmes!

Surprisingly, then, he was anything but Bohemian in what he wore. The "catlike love of personal cleanliness" was reflected in "a certain quiet primness of dress."

He customarily wore tweeds or a formal long frock coat when out of Baker Street. When the weather called for it, he would wear an ulster as an overcoat. On his frequent visits to the country he preferred "a long gray travelling-cloak" (an Inverness) and with it a close-fitting cloth cap with ear flaps. It is this article of headwear that has become confused—through various illustrations—with the 'deerstalker'—in much the same way as the meerschaum became the visual synonym for 'pipe.'

[The blame for the meerschaum can be laid fairly and squarely at the door of actor William Gillette, who played Holmes on stage for many years. He found it too difficult to enunciate his lines with a straight-stemmed pipe in his mouth. The meerschaum was easier! Thus are legends born.]

Once back at 221B, it was invariably off with the jacket and on with the dressing gown. He owned at least three of them and each appears to have been worn to fit a suitable mood or purpose—again, in much the same way as his various pipes. There was a purple one, worn at breakfast, a blue one and the famous "mouse-coloured" one (dark gray with a hint of yellow) that was also used to dress the wax figure of Holmes used as a decoy in "The Empty

House." As soon as Holmes returns after the capture of Colonel Moran, he dons it himself, suggesting, perhaps, that it was in this one that he felt most at home.

* * * *

From time to time Watson was inclined to refer to his accounts as being a "somewhat incoherent series." While he did himself less than justice by such a self-deprecating comment, there are—it must be admitted—a number of observations concerning his friend that are, to say the least, inconsistent.

For instance, he was far too quick to dismiss Holmes's feeling about the great outdoors. Certainly, in pessimistic mood the detective was capable of looking at the countryside and sensing the latent evil beneath the beauty—but it was the evil mankind brought to everything he touched that was his real concern. Watson was overstating the case when he wrote in "The Reigate Squires" that

"Neither the country nor the sea presented the slightest attraction to him. He loved to lie in the centre of five millions of people, with his filaments stretching out and running through them, responsive to every little rumour or suspicion of unsolved crime. Appreciation of Nature found no place among his many gifts and his only change was when he turned his mind from the evildoer of the town to track down his brother of the country."

Or perhaps his wandering during the Great Hiatus opened Holmes's eyes to other possibilities. Certainly, by the time of "Black Peter" (1895) he can suggest to Watson . . .

"Let us walk in these beautiful woods, Watson, and give a few hours to the birds and flowers."

Even so, it is surprising that Watson—who, as Holmes remarked, was given to putting "colour and life" into each of his

"Holmes spent much of his time in long walks and solitary meditations."
(Gilbert Holiday for "The Devil's Foot," 1910)

statements—did not recall that as early as *The Sign of Four* his friend had waxed lyrical on the subject at least once:

"How sweet the morning air! See how that one little cloud floats like a pink feather from some gigantic flamingo ... How small we feel, with our petty ambitions and strivings in the presence of the great elemental forces of Nature!"

"'What a lovely thing a rose is!'

"He walked past the couch to the open window and held up the drooping stalk of a moss-rose, looking down at the dainty blend of crimson and green. It was a new phase of his character to me, for I had never before seen him show any keen interest in natural objects.

'For highest assurance of the goodness of Providence seems to me to rest in the flowers. All other things, our powers, our desires, our food, are all really necessary for our existence in the first instance. But this rose is an extra. Its smell and its colour are an embellishment of life, not a condition of it. It is only goodness which gives extras, and so I say again that we have much to hope for from the flowers.'" ("The Naval Treaty")

"Of late I have been tempted to look into the problems of nature." ("The Final Problem")

"It is very pleasant to see the first green shoots upon the hedges and the catkins on the hazels once again. With a spud, a tin box, and an elementary book on botany, there are instructive days to be spent." ("Wisteria Lodge")

And particularly in retirement ...

"On the morning of which I speak the wind had abated, and all Nature was newly washed and fresh. It was impossible to work upon so delightful a day, and I strolled out before breakfast to enjoy the exquisite air." ("The Lion's Mane")

... something he could hardly have done in Baker Street! Or in *A Study in Scarlet* ...

"What a lovely thing a rose is." (Sidney Paget for "The Naval Treaty," 1893)

"One's ideas must be as broad as Nature if they are to interpret Nature."

Incidentally, the very title of the case—taken from Holmes's own description of the case, "our Study in Scarlet . . . Why shouldn't we use a little art jargon . . . the scarlet thread of murder running through the colourless skein of life"—was, in itself, atypically poetic for him and an ironic reference to the American painter James McNeill Whistler's simplistic habit of titling his various paintings a "Study in . . ." this or that colour. His best known work—popularly called "Whistler's Mother"—was "A Study in Black and Grey."

* * * *

Holmes was not given to philosophizing but every now and again—usually at the end of a case and always alone with Watson—he would speculate on matters which were not capable of scientific appraisal . . .

"Life is infinitely stranger than anything which the mind of man could invent. We would not dare to conceive the things which are really mere commonplaces of existence. If we could fly out of that window hand in hand, hover over this great city, gently remove the roofs, and peep in at the queer things which are going on, the strange coincidences, the plannings, the cross-purposes, the wonderful chains of events, working through generations, and leading to the most outré results, it would make all fiction with its conventionalities and foreseen conclusions most stale and unprofitable." ("A Case of Identity")

"Amid the action and reaction of so dense a swarm of humanity, every possible combination of events may be expected to take place." ("The Blue Carbuncle")

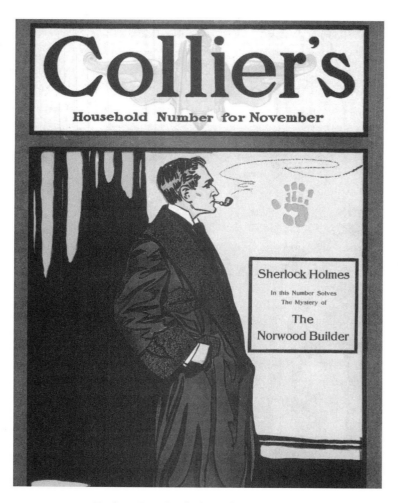

Frederic Dorr Steele for *Collier's Magazine*

Although he was not often articulate on the subject, Holmes would occasionally say something that indicated that, at heart, he believed devoutly in aspects of progress and the democratic process.

In "The Naval Treaty" Holmes and Watson are returning to London by train. As they pass Clapham Junction, Holmes remarks: "It's a very cheering thing to come into London by any of these lines which run high and allow you to look down upon houses like this."

I thought he was joking, for the view was sordid enough, but he soon explained himself.

'Look at those big, isolated clumps of buildings rising up above the slates, like brick islands in a lead-coloured sea.'

'The Board schools.'

'Lighthouses, my boy! Beacons of the future! Capsules, with hundreds of bright little seeds in each, out of which will spring the wiser, better England of the future.'"

In most of his observations, though, he was inclined to the melancholic . . .

"The ways of Fate are indeed hard to understand. If there is not some compensation hereafter, then the world is a cruel jest . . . The example of patient suffering is in itself the most precious of all lessons to an impatient world." ("The Veiled Lodger")

"But is not all life pathetic and futile? Is not his story a microcosm of the whole? We reach. We grasp. And what is left in our hands at the end? A shadow. Or worse than a shadow—misery." ("The Retired Colourman")

. . . although he was prepared to consider a more pragmatic verdict . . .

"What you do in this world is a matter of no consequence. The question is, what can you make people believe you have done." (*A Study in Scarlet*)

And if that statement (made in 1887) has a familiar ring to it, it's because Oscar Wilde said—"What is true in a man's life is not what he does but the legend which grows up around him" . . .

"I wish I'd said that." 'You *will*, Oscar, you *will!*'"

* * * *

There remains the mystery of The Great Hiatus (May 1891–1894). Not the *fact* of it—that was obvious enough—but the *how* of it.

On his dramatic return in "The Empty House" Holmes appears anxious to brief Watson on his movements during those three years.

After his escape from the Reichenbach Falls he went to Florence . . . then "travelled for two years in Tibet . . . and amused myself by visiting Lhassa (The Forbidden City) and spending some time with the head Llama . . ."

[Many Holmes scholars have made heavy-handed fun at Holmes's expense over the misspelling of 'lama,' pointing out that Holmes must have 'amused himself by conversing with a furry four-footed animal from the Andes.' The point, surely, is that—as so often—what we hear from Holmes is recounted by Watson, so presumably the spelling mistake is Watson's.]

"You may have read of the remarkable explorations of a Norwegian called Sigerson but I am sure that it never occurred to you that you were receiving news of your friend."

[This, too, is an atypical passage for Holmes, who is not normally given to hyperbole in describing his own achievements and suggests, at best, that he is reciting a speech that he had carefully prepared in advance.]

Holmes and Watson at home in Baker Street. (Sidney Paget from *The Strand* magazine)

"I then passed through Persia, looking in at Mecca ..." [Another phrase that belongs more properly on a holiday postcard.]

" ... and paid a short but interesting visit to the Khalifa at Khartoum, the results of which I have communicated to the Foreign Office ..."

[The clue to the whole prolonged absence, one suspects, may lie right here. A Sherlock Holmes, free for the first time from public scrutiny and funded by his brother Mycroft—the only person to know the true situation—would have been the ideal secret agent for the British government in a world rapidly turning troublesome for the Empire. That "interesting visit to the Khalifa" was almost certainly the admissible tip of a much larger iceberg. The idea of Sigerson/Holmes as 007 with Mycroft as 'M' makes for interesting speculation.]

"Returning to France, I spent some months in research into the coal-tar derivatives, which I conducted in a laboratory at Montpellier [another Watson misspelling for 'Montpelier'] in the south of France." [Again, isn't Holmes providing too much excess detail? Even Watson could be expected to know that Montpelier was in the South of France.]

At this point in time we are most unlikely to ever know all that Holmes did during his 'sabbatical' but it would surely be reasonable to speculate that he went further and achieved more than he was either able or prepared to admit to Watson on that day in May 1894.

Did he, perhaps, take a trip to the United States and make (or renew) the professional acquaintance of Wilson Hargreave and his colleagues at the New York Police Department? If so, he must have adopted an alias and revealed his true identity later before Hargreaves "made use of my knowledge of London crime."

Whatever he did, we can be sure that he never stopped storing useful knowledge away in that little 'brain-attic' of his mind, ready for the day when it would be needed.

"My Brother Mycroft"

M YCROFT HOLMES was seven years Holmes's senior and by the time we meet him, high up in Government circles. Since it would have been inconceivable in those days for anyone to be accepted without a suitable 'background,' it strongly suggests that Mycroft's education, at the very least, was more formal than Sherlock's—probably a recognized public school, followed by Oxford or Cambridge.

Much to Watson's surprise, Holmes is adamant that Mycroft's deductive abilities significantly exceed his own:

"I cannot agree with those who rank modesty among the virtues. To the logician all things should be seen exactly as they are, and to underestimate one's self is as much a departure from truth as to exaggerate one's powers. When I say, therefore, that Mycroft has better powers of observation than I, you may take it that I am speaking the exact and literal truth . . . If the art of the detective began and ended in reasoning from an armchair, my brother would be the greatest criminal agent that ever lived. But he has no ambition and no energy. He will not even go out

Mycroft Holmes. (Sidney Paget for "The Greek Interpreter," 1893)

of his way to verify his own solutions, and would rather be considered wrong than take the trouble to prove himself right. Again and again I have taken a problem to him and have received an explanation which has afterwards proved to be the correct one. And yet he was absolutely incapable of working out the practical points which must be gone into before a case could be laid before a judge or jury . . . What is to me a means of livelihood is to him the merest hobby of a dilettante."

Mycroft has an anonymous role in government—but Holmes informs Watson with some pride—"You would also be right in a sense if you said that occasionally he *is* the British Government."

"(He) draws four hundred and fifty pounds a year, remains a subordinate, has no ambitions of any kind, will receive neither honour nor title, but remains the most indispensable man in the country . . .

"Well, his position is unique. He has made it for himself. There has never been anything like it before; nor will be again. He has the tidiest and most orderly brain, with the greatest capacity for storing facts, of any man living. The same great powers which I have turned to the detection of crime he has used for this particular business. The conclusions of every department are passed to him, and he is the central exchange, the clearing-house, which makes out the balance. All other men are specialists, but his specialism is omniscience. We will suppose that a Minister needs information as to a point which involves the Navy, India, Canada and the bi-metallic question; he could get his separate advices from various departments upon each, but only Mycroft can focus them all, and say offhand how each factor would affect the other. They began by using him as a short-cut, a convenience; now he has made himself an essential. In that great brain of his everything is pigeon-holed, and can be handed out in an instant. Again and again his word has decided the national policy. He lives in it. He thinks of nothing else save when, as an intellectual exercise, he unbends if I call upon him and ask him to advise me on one of my little problems." ("The Bruce-Partington Plans")

*   *   *   *

In physique Mycroft was a marked contrast to Holmes. When Watson first meets him in "The Greek Interpreter" he finds "a much larger and stouter man than Sherlock. His body was absolutely corpulent, but his face, though massive, had preserved something of the sharpness of expression which was so remarkable in that of his brother. His eyes, which were of a peculiarly light, watery gray, seemed to always retain that far-away, introspective look which I had only observed in Sherlock's when he was exerting his full powers."

Seven years later—at the time of the adventure of "The Bruce-Partington Plans"—he was to amplify that first impression:

"Heavily built and massive, there was a suggestion of uncouth physical inertia in the figure, but above this unwieldy frame there was perched a head so masterful in its brow, so alert in its steel-grey, deep-set eyes, so firm in its lips, and so subtle in its play of expression, that after the first glance one forgot the gross body and remembered only the dominant mind."

When Holmes hears that his brother is to pay a visit to him in Baker Street, he is clearly shocked by the news:

"Mycroft lodges in Pall Mall, and he walks around the corner into Whitehall every morning and back every evening. From year's end to year's end he takes no other exercise, and is seen nowhere else, except only in the Diogenes Club, which is just opposite his rooms."

"It is as if you met a tram-car coming down a country lane. Mycroft has his rails and he runs on them. His Pall Mall lodgings, the Diogenes Club, Whitehall—that is his cycle. Once, and only once, he has been here." ("The Greek Interpreter") What upheaval can possibly have derailed him? "A planet might as well leave its orbit." Later he changes the analogy to mythology—"Jupiter (the King of the gods) is descending."

"'Come in,' said he, blandly." (Sidney Paget for "The Greek Interpreter,"
1893)

"The tall and portly form of Mycroft Holmes was ushered into the room."
(Arthur Twidle for "The Bruce-Partington Plans," 1908)

Mycroft had been a founding member of the Diogenes Club, "some little distance from the Carlton (Club)"—named after the fourth century b.c. Greek philosopher who lived a life of voluntary poverty. As they travel there to meet Mycroft for the first time, Holmes explains the club's rather exotic origins . . .

"The Diogenes Club is the queerest club in London, and Mycroft one of the queerest men . . . He's always there from quarter to five to twenty to eight."

"There are many men in London, you know, who, some from shyness, some from misanthropy, have no wish for the company of their fellows. Yet they are not averse to comfortable chairs and the latest periodicals. It is for the convenience of these that the Diogenes Club was started, and now it contains the most unsociable and unclubable men in town. No member is permitted to take the least notice of any other one. Save in the Stranger's Room, no talking is, under any circumstances, allowed, and three offences, if brought to the notice of the committee, render the talker liable to expulsion. My brother was one of the founders, and I have myself found it a very soothing atmosphere."

Although Mycroft was only involved in two of the cases recorded by Watson, he played an important part in Holmes's escape from London in "The Final Problem," being the anonymous cab driver who took them to the railway station. And, of course, it was he who—much to Watson's subsequent distress—was Holmes's sole confidant during the Great Hiatus of 1891–1894. Mycroft provided Holmes with funds during that period and paid the rent on 221B, with the instruction to Mrs. Hudson that Holmes's rooms should be kept precisely as he had left them.

As Holmes reminded Watson on his return ("The Empty House") . . . "You will realise that among your many talents dissimulation finds no place" and, knowing Moriarty's men would be watching Watson, his old friend's distress was an integral part of his deception. "The features are given to a man as the means by which he shall express his emotions, and yours are faithful servants." ("The Resident Patient")

As a professional civil servant, presumably brother Mycroft could be relied upon to dissemble effectively indefinitely.

"You Know My Methods"

"You know my method. It is founded upon the observance of trifles . . . Observation and inference. Therein lies my métier."

—"The Boscombe Valley Mystery"

"My name is Sherlock Holmes. It is my business to know what other people don't know."

—"The Blue Carbuncle"

"It is my business to know things. Perhaps I have trained myself to see what others have overlooked." —"A Case of Identity" . . . "That is my trade." —"The Blanched Soldier"

"You know my methods. Apply them."

—The Sign of Four

"Crime is common. Logic is rare."

—"The Copper Beeches"

*   *   *   *

"They say that genius is an infinite capacity for taking pains. It's a very bad definition, but it does apply to detective work." (*A Study in Scarlet*)

As he got to know the remarkable man whose life he was vicariously sharing—and which he soon began chronicling . . .

"'It is wonderful!' I cried.'Your merits should be publicly recognised. You should publish an account of the case. If you won't, I will for you.'

'You may do what you like, Doctor,' he answered." (*A Study in Scarlet*)

Watson soon began to appreciate that Holmes was a man of unique abilities:

"You have brought detection as near an exact science as it will ever be brought in this world." (*A Study in Scarlet*)

". . . from all you have told me, it seems obvious that your faculty of observation and your peculiar facility for deduction are due to your own systematic training." ("The Greek Interpreter")

He rapidly became, in fact, "the most incisive reasoner and most energetic agent in Europe". . . "unofficial adviser and helper to everybody who is absolutely puzzled, throughout three continents" And, looking back in 1901, Watson would conclude that "It is safe to say that there was no public case of any difficulty in which he was not consulted during those eight years (1894–1901) and there were hundreds of private cases, some of them of the most intricate and extraordinary character, in which he played a prominent part. Many startling successes and a few unavoidable failures were the outcome of this long period of continuous work." ("The Solitary Cyclist")

Shortly after the two men first met, Holmes explained the solid basis of his approach to his chosen profession:

"I have a turn both for observation and deduction. The theories are extremely practical—so practical that I depend on them for my bread and cheese . . . I have a trade of my own. I suppose I am the

"Is there any other point which I can make clear?" (Sidney Paget for "The Naval Treaty," 1893)

only one in the world. I'm a consulting detective . . . Here in London we have lots of Government detectives and lots of private ones. When these fellows are at fault, they come to me, and I manage to put them on the right scent. They lay all the evidence before me, and I am able, by the help of my knowledge of the history of crime, to set them straight. There is a strong family resemblance about misdeeds, and if you have all the details of a thousand at your finger ends, it is odd if you can't unravel the thousand and first . . . I have a kind of intuition . . . Observation to me is second nature."

"As a rule, when I have heard some slight indication of the course of events I am able to guide myself by the thousands of similar cases which occur to my memory." ("The Red-Headed League")

"All knowledge is useful to a detective," he believed, and once advised Inspector MacDonald—"Mr. Mac, the most practical thing that you ever did in your life would be to shut yourself up for three months and read twelve hours a day at the annals of crime. Everything comes in circles . . . The old wheel turns, and the same spoke comes up. It's all been done before, and will be again." (*The Valley of Fear*)

With this early understanding, Watson was able to observe—though not deduce—as case succeeded case, how Holmes's "rapid deductions, as swift as intuitions" were, in fact, "always founded on a logical basis" and how "minute and laborious investigations . . . formed the solid basis on which his brilliant edifices of deduction were reared." ("The Abbey Grange")

To be fair, there were failures. "I have been beaten by three men and one woman" (Irene Adler) . . . "Some cases have baffled his analytical skill . . . while others have been but partially cleared up and have their explanations founded rather upon conjecture than on that absolutely logical proof that was so dear to him."

"I could see by Holmes's face that he was much puzzled." (Sidney Paget for "The Abbey Grange," 1904)

The man's mind was truly remarkable in its ability to focus . . .

"I find that a concentrated atmosphere helps a concentration of thought. I have not pushed it to the length of getting into a box to think, but that is the logical outcome of my convictions." (*The Hound of the Baskervilles*)

. . . and, equally, to turn itself off . . .

"One of the most remarkable characteristics . . . was his power of throwing his brain out of action and switching all his thoughts on to lighter things whenever he had convinced himself that he could no longer work to advantage." ("The Bruce-Partington Plans")

Holmes was well aware that he was merely a vehicle that happened to house a valuable piece of mental machinery . . .

"My mind is like a racing engine, tearing itself to pieces" . . . when "it is not connected up with the work for which it was built . . ." ("Wisteria Lodge") . . . "To let the brain work without sufficient material is like racing an engine. It racks itself to pieces." ("The Devil's Foot")

"I am a brain, Watson. The rest of me is a mere appendix." ("The Mazarin Stone")

*   *   *   *

"The world is full of obvious things which nobody by any chance ever observes." (*The Hound of the Baskervilles*)

It was a lesson that Holmes was to din into Watson throughout their long association.

Handwriting, for instance, could reveal a great deal to the trained eye. "You may not be aware that the deduction of a man's age from his writing is one which has been brought to a considerable accuracy by experts. In normal cases one can place a man in his true decade with tolerable confidence." ("The Reigate Squires")

"Holding it only an inch or two before his eyes." (Sidney Paget for *The Hound of the Baskervilles*, 1901)

"I see no more than you, but I have trained myself to notice what I see." ("The Blanched Soldier") . . . "I see it, I deduce it. You see, but you do not observe." ("A Scandal in Bohemia") . . . "You can see everything. You fail, however, to reason from what you see. You are too timid in drawing your inferences." ("The Blue Carbuncle")

Clues were "not invisible but unnoticed . . . You did not know where to look, and so you missed all that was important. I can never bring you to realise the importance of sleeves, the suggestiveness of thumbnails or the great issues that may hang from a bootlace." ("A Case of Identity")

Which was probably just as well—or there may soon have been an independent organization called 'J. H. Watson—Consulting Detective.'

Holmes never ceased to regard Watson as a potential pupil. One of the first lessons was to accumulate one's data . . .

"Data! Data! Data! I can't make bricks without clay." ("The Noble Bachelor") . . . "I have no data yet. It is a capital mistake to theorise before one has data. Insensibly one begins to twist facts to suit theories, instead of theories to suit facts." ("A Scandal in Bohemia") . . . "I never guess. It is a shocking habit—destructive to the logical faculty . . . I never make exceptions. An exception disproves the rule." (*The Sign of Four*)

Nonetheless, he did admit at least once—"I suspect myself of coming to conclusions too rapidly." ("The Naval Treaty")

Even apparent 'facts' were there to be questioned before they were accepted as such . . .

"Never trust to general impressions . . . but concentrate yourself upon details." ("A Case of Identity") . . . "Circumstantial evidence is a very tricky thing; it may seem to point very straight to one thing, but if you shift your point of view a little, you may find it pointing in an equally uncompromising manner to something entirely different." ("The

Boscombe Valley Mystery") "When once your point of view is changed, the very thing which was so damning becomes a clue to the truth." ("Thor Bridge") . . . "I ought to know by this time that when a fact appears to be opposed to a long train of deductions it invariably proves to be capable of some other interpretation." (A *Study in Scarlet*). . . "It may well be that several explanations remain, in which case one tries test after test until one or other of them has a convincing amount of support." ("The Blanched Soldier") "When you follow two separate trains of thought, you will find some point of intersection which should approximate to the truth." ("Lady Frances Carfax")

Simplify, simplify, simplify . . .

"Eliminate all other factors, and the one which remains must be the truth". . . "How often have I said to you that when you have eliminated the impossible, whatever remains, however improbable, must be the truth?" (*The Sign of Four*)

It was vital—in Holmes's view—to begin a case with one's mind wiped clean of any preconceptions . . .

"I make a point of never having any prejudices, and of following docilely wherever fact may lead me." ("The Reigate Squires") . . . "We approached the case with an absolutely blank mind, which is always an advantage. We had formed no theories. We were simply there to observe and to draw inferences from our observations." ("The Cardboard Box") . . . "We imagined what might have happened, acted upon the supposition, and find ourselves justified." ("The Speckled Band")

Despite his many successes, though, Holmes was ultimately despondent about the prospects for his unique skills . . .

"Pshaw, my dear fellow, what do the public, the great unobservant public, who could hardly tell a weaver by his tooth or a compositor by his left thumb, care about the finer shades of analysis or deduction?" ("The Copper Beeches")

* * * *

One of Holmes's favorite party pieces was to surprise a client—
and invariably Watson—by his apparent clairvoyance . . .

"'Beyond the obvious facts that he has at some time done man-
ual labour, that he takes snuff, that he is a Freemason, that he has been
in China, and that he has done a considerable amount of writing lately,
I can deduce nothing else.'"

"'Excellent!' I cried.

'Elementary,' said he. It is one of those instances where the reasoner can produce an effect which seems remarkable to his neigh-
bour, because the latter has missed the one little point which is the
basis of the deduction." ("The Crooked Man")

"'Now, Watson, confess yourself utterly taken aback.' said he.

'I am.'

'I ought to make you sign a paper to that effect.'

'Why?'

'Because in five minutes you will say that it is all so absurdly simple.'" ("The Noble Bachelor")

"Every mystery is simple once it is explained."

. . . a point which Holmes is at pains to demonstrate to Inspector
Gregson in the adventure of "Silver Blaze." Gregson asks him . . .

"'Is there any point to which you would wish to draw my attention?'

'To the curious incident of the dog in the night-time.'

'The dog did nothing in the night-time.'

'That was the curious incident.'"

Holmes was always fond of the cryptic utterance . . .

"'I followed you.'

'I saw no one.'

'That is what you may expect to see when I follow you.'" ("The
Devil's Foot")

* * * *

The power of reason was paramount to Holmes. . .

"The ideal reasoner would, when he has once been shown a single fact in all its bearings, deduce from it not only all the chain of events which led up to it, but also all the results which would follow from it. As Cuvier [Georges Cuvier (1769–1832) was the French naturalist who pioneered the study of comparative anatomy and paleontology] could correctly describe a whole animal by the contemplation of a single bone, so the observer who has thoroughly understood one link in a series of incidents, should be able accurately to state all the other ones, both before and after. We have not yet grasped the results which the reason alone can attain to. Problems may be solved in the study which have baffled all those who sought a solution by the aid of their senses. To carry the art, however, to its highest pitch, it is necessary that the reasoner should be able to utilise all the facts which have come to his knowledge, which, even in these days of education and encyclopaedias, is a somewhat rare accomplishment. It is not so impossible, however, that a man should possess all knowledge that is likely to be useful to him in his work, and this I have endeavoured in my case to do." ("The Five Orange Pips")

"The grand thing is to be able to reason backwards. That is a very useful accomplishment, and a very easy one, but people do not practice it much. In the everyday affairs of life it is more useful to reason forwards . . . Most people, if you describe a train of events to them, will tell you what the result would be. They can put those events together in their minds, and argue from them that something will come to pass. There are few people, however, who, if you told them a result, would be able to evolve from their own inner consciousness what the steps were which led up to that result. This power is what I mean when I talk of reasoning backwards, or analytically." (A Study in Scarlet)

"Holmes…smelled the single cigar it contained." (Sidney Paget for "The Resident Patient," 1893)

"I cannot guarantee that I carry all the facts in my mind. Intense mental concentration has a curious way of blotting out what has passed. The barrister who has his case at his fingers' ends and is able to argue with an expert upon his own subject finds that a week or two of the courts will drive it all out of his head once more. So each of my cases displaces the last." (*The Hound of the Baskervilles*)

* * * *

In applying that thinking Holmes had perfected a number of specific techniques.

When Watson first encounters him, Holmes has just perfected a test to detect the presence of bloodstains and is jubilant . . .

"Why, man, it is the most practical medico-legal discovery for years. Don't you see that it gives us an infallible test for blood stains . . . There was the case of Von Bischoff at Frankfurt last year. He would certainly have been hung had this test been in existence. Then there was Mason of Radford, and the notorious Muller, and Lefevre of Montpellier, and Samson of New Orleans. I could name a score of cases in which it would have been decisive." (*A Study in Scarlet*)

One of the first things he liked to examine was someone's foot . . .

"There is no branch of detective science which is so important and so much neglected as the art of tracing footsteps." . . . "The height of a man, in nine cases out of ten, can be told from the length of his stride. It is a simple calculation enough . . ." (*A Study in Scarlet*)

Of course, one must guard against an opponent—like Holmes himself—clever enough to understand the rules and break them . . . "I might have reversed by boots, as I have done on similar occasions." ("The Empty House")

"Pipes are occasionally of extraordinary interest. Nothing has more individuality, save perhaps watches and bootlaces." ("The Yellow Face")

"It would be difficult to name any articles which afford a finer field for inference than a pair of glasses." ("The Golden Pince-Nez")

"I am familiar with forty-two different impressions left by tyres." ("The Priory School")

"There are seventy-five perfumes, which it is very necessary that a criminal expert should be able to distinguish from each other, and cases have more than once within my own experience depended upon their prompt recognition." (*The Hound of the Baskervilles*)

Then there was the question of typography . . .

"There is as much difference to my eyes between the leaded bourgeois type of a *Times* article and the slovenly print of an evening halfpenny paper as there could be between your Negro and your Esquimaux. The detection of type is one of the most elementary branches of knowledge to the special expert in crime, though I confess that once when I was very young I confused a *Leeds Mercury* with the *Western Morning News*." (*The Hound of the Baskervilles*)

The 'special expert' also needed to know the geography of his terrain at least as well as a taxi driver . . . "It is a hobby of mine to have an exact knowledge of London." ("The Red-Headed League") And in Holmes's case to have a number of 'safe houses'—five, in fact—dotted around the metropolis, so that he could dart into one and elude possible pursuit by emerging as someone completely different.

"Holmes's knowledge of the by-ways of London was extraordinary, and on this occasion he passed rapidly, with an assured step, through a network of mews and stables the very existence of which I had never known." ("The Empty House")

"In rapid succession we passed through the fringe of fashionable London, hotel London, theatrical London, literary London, commercial

Holmes studies the cipher. (Frank Wiles for *The Valley of Fear*, 1914)

London and, finally, maritime London, till we came to a river-side city of a hundred thousand souls, where the tenement houses swelter and reek with the outcasts of Europe." ("The Six Napoleons")

The London of Holmes and Watson's day was a very different city from the relatively unpolluted neon jungle of today. Watson describes it with perceptive—almost poetic—skill, as he, Holmes and Mary Morstan wait outside the Lyceum Theatre to meet their mysterious contact one autumn evening in 1888 . . .

"It was a September evening and not yet seven o'clock, but the day had been a dreary one, and a dense drizzly fog lay low upon the great city. Mud-coloured clouds drooped sadly over the muddy streets. Down the Strand the lamps were but misty splotches of diffused light, which threw a feeble circular glimmer upon the slimy pavement. The yellow glare from the shop-windows streamed out into the steamy, vaporous air, and threw a murky, shifting radiance across the crowded thoroughfare. There was, to my mind, something eerie and ghost-like in the endless procession of faces which flitted across these narrow bars of light." (*The Sign of Four*)

In such a London the possibilities for the criminal predator were limitless.

"Look out of this window, Watson. See how the figures loom up, are dimly seen, and then blend once more into the cloud-bank. The thief or the murderer could roam London on such a day as the tiger does the jungle, unseen until he pounces, and then evident only to his victim." ("The Bruce-Partington Plans")

Pope may have pre-empted Holmes by asserting that "the proper study of mankind is man" and Wordsworth by claiming that "The Child is father of the man" but Holmes took the dictum an important practical stage further: "I have frequently gained my first real insight into the character of parents by studying their children." ("The Noble Bachelor")

And when it came to questioning witnesses . . . "He was a past master in the art of putting a humble witness at his ease.". . .

"The main thing is never to let them think that their information can be of the slightest importance to you. If you do, they will instantly shut up like an oyster. If you listen to them under protest, as it were, you are very likely to get what you want." (*The Sign of Four*)

* * * *

But none of these techniques or any others was a substitute for first accurately defining the problem.

"It is of the highest importance in the art of detection to be able to recognise, out of a number of facts, which are incidental and which vital, otherwise your energy and attention must be dissipated, instead of concentrated." ("The Reigate Squires")

Over the years he refined a number of axioms to guide the detective.

"It is a mistake to confound strangeness with mystery. The most commonplace crime is often the most mysterious, because it presents no new or special features from which deductions may be drawn." (*A Study in Scarlet*) . . . "Just as a commonplace face is the most difficult to identify." ("The Red-Headed League") . . . "As a rule the more bizarre a thing is the less mysterious it proves to be." ("The Red-Headed League") . . . "Depend upon it, there is nothing so unnatural as the commonplace." ("A Case of Identity") . . . "There is nothing more deceptive than an obvious fact . . . Singularity is almost invariably a clue." ("The Boscombe Valley Mystery") . . . "The strangest and most unique things are very often connected . . . with the smaller crimes." ("The Red-Headed League") . . . "The more *outré* and grotesque an incident is the more carefully it deserves to be examined, and the very point which appears to complicate the case is, when duly considered and scientifically handled, the one which is most likely to elucidate it." (*The Hound of the Baskervilles*) . . . "I have found that it is usually in unimportant matters that there is a field for observation". . . "It has long been an axiom of mine that the little things are infinitely the most important . . . the gravest issues may depend upon the smallest things.". . . "To a great mind, nothing is little." (*A Study in Scarlet*)

"I dare call nothing trivial when I reflect that some of my most classic cases have had the least promising commencement." ("The Six Napoleons")

* * * *

Several of Holmes's cases appeared—at least initially—to involve aspects of the supernatural, but Holmes would have none of it . . .

"This Agency stands flat-footed upon the ground, and there it must remain. The world is big enough. No ghosts need apply." ("The Sussex Vampire") . . . "I fear . . . that if the matter is beyond humanity it is certainly beyond me." ("The Devil's Foot")

"I have investigated many crimes, but I have never yet seen one which was committed by a flying creature. As long as the criminal remains upon two legs so long must there be some indentation, some abrasion, some trifling displacement which can be detected by the scientific researcher." ("Black Peter")

"I have hitherto confined my investigations to this world. In a modest way I have combated evil, but to take on the Father of Evil himself would, perhaps, be too ambitious a task." (*The Hound of the Baskervilles*)

The paranormal was beyond his personal pale, but . . .

"I admit mere imagination, but how often is imagination the mother of truth?" (*The Valley of Fear*)

Scientific use of the imagination, he felt, was "the region where we balance the probabilities and choose the most likely!"

. . . and at the outset of their working relationship in *A Study in Scarlet* he provided Watson with a definition of the business they would be engaged in . . .

"There is a mystery about this that stimulates the imagination; where there is no imagination there is no horror."

Nonetheless—until proved to be in error—Sherlock Holmes would continue to believe that every problem had lurking within it a rational explanation waiting to be released—and the most intriguing were all around us:

"For strange effects and extraordinary combinations we must go to life itself, which is always far more daring than any effort of the imagination." ("The Red-Headed League")

But despite his considerable powers, he was always the supreme realist about those powers. "The past and the present are within the field of my inquiry, but what a man may do in the future is a hard question to answer." (*The Hound of the Baskervilles*)

* * * *

"The best way of successfully acting a part is to be it." ("The Dying Detective")

If a criminal were being pursued by Holmes, he might see no one—or he might see someone entirely different. For the man was a master of disguise . . .

"It was not merely that Holmes changed his costume. His expression, his manner, his very soul seemed to vary with every fresh part he assumed. The stage lost a fine actor, just as science lost an acute reasoner, when he became a specialist in crime." ("A Scandal in Bohemia")

Sherlock Holmes as "a drunken-looking groom." (Sidney Paget for "A Scandal in Bohemia," 1891)

In *A Study in Scarlet* Watson—who had yet to become accustomed to his friend's habit of changing his persona—does not recognize "an aged man, clad in seafaring garb, with an old pea-jacket buttoned up to his throat. His back was bowed, his knees were shaky and his breathing was painfully asthmatic. He had a (red) coloured scarf round his chin and I could see little of his face save a pair of keen dark eyes, overhung by bushy white eyebrows and long grey sidewhiskers. Altogether he gave me the impression of a respectable master mariner who had fallen into years and poverty."

When Holmes reveals himself, Inspector Athelney Jones compliments him—"Ah, you rogue! . . . You would have made an actor, and a rare one. You had the proper workhouse cough, and those weak legs of yours are worth ten pounds a week."

In "A Scandal in Bohemia" he was first "a drunken-looking groom, ill-kempt and side-whiskered with an inflamed face and disreputable clothes," then "an amiable and simple-minded Nonconformist clergyman. His broad black hat, his baggy trousers, his white tie, his sympathetic smile and general look of peering and benevolent curiosity" deceive Watson all over again.

In point of fact, although he can later claim—"Accustomed as I was to my friend's amazing powers in the use of disguises," Watson *never* succeeds in penetrating a single one of them—even though Holmes clearly advises him that "It is the first quality of a criminal investigator that he should see through a disguise."

. . . "an old man, very thin, wrinkled, bent with age (and) doddering, loose-lipped senility" ("The Man with the Twisted Lip")

. . . a "common loafer, with his collar turned up, his shiny seedy coat, his red cravat and his worn boots, he was a perfect sample of the class"—so much so that Holmes can hardly wait "to get these disreputable clothes off and return to my highly respectable self." ("The Blue Carbuncle")

"A common loafer." (Sidney Paget for "The Beryl Coronet," 1892)

"A simple-minded clergyman." (Sidney Paget for
"A Scandal in Bohemia," 1891)

One of his more dramatic impersonations, of course, was in "The Empty House," when he appears to Watson as "an elderly deformed book collector . . . his sharp, wizened face peering out from a frame of white hair" and offering such collector's items as *The Origin of Tree Worship*, *The Holy War*, *British Birds*, and *Catullus*. When he abandons the part—causing Watson to faint at the sight of Holmes apparently returned from the grave—having assured himself that his friend is recovering . . . "I have given you a serious shock by my unnecessarily dramatic reappearance." Holmes's concern is primarily for his own comfort: "I am glad to stretch myself. It is no joke when a tall man has to take a foot off his stature for several hours on end."

"A venerable Italian priest with broken English" appears in "The Final Problem." "The aged ecclesiastic had turned his face towards me. For an instant the wrinkles were smoothed away, the nose drew away from the chin, the lower lip ceased to protrude and the mouth to mumble, the dull eyes regained their fire, the drooping figure expanded. Then next the whole frame collapsed again, and Holmes had gone as quickly as he had come."

In "Black Peter" Holmes became 'Captain Basil'—a gentleman we are never privileged to meet—while in "The Disappearance of Lady Frances Carfax" he was "an unshaven French *ouvrier* in a blue blouse"—and in "The Mazarin Stone" both "a workman looking for a job" and "an old woman" with a "baggy parasol." ("I was never more convincing," he tells Watson.)

Unless, of course, it was as the "rakish young workman with a goatee beard and a swagger" who "lit his clay pipe at the lamp." It was as "Escott, a plumber with a rising business" that he wooed and won the heart and hand of Milverton's housemaid in "Charles Augustus Milverton"—surely his ultimate triumph.

On two occasions (that we know of) Holmes succeeded in deceiving opponents by disguising himself as—himself.

"I knocked down several books that he was carrying." (Sidney Paget for
"The Empty House," 1903)

"My decrepit Italian friend." (Sidney Paget for "The Final Problem," 1893)

In "The Empty House" it is the wax bust of Holmes by Oscar Meunier of Grenoble sitting in the window of 221b that attracted the attention of Colonel Moran and his henchman. The likeness was so great that when Watson first sees it, he "threw out his hand to make sure that the man himself was standing beside him."

Holmes repeats the stratagem in "The Mazarin Stone"—this time with a dummy made by Tavernier, the French modeler.

Presumably Holmes had thought it prudent not to inform M. Meunier of the fate of his original creation. Presumably, also, Count Silvius (his adversary in the latter story) had omitted to read Watson's account of "The Empty House."

* * * *

Disguise was all part of Holmes's innate sense of the dramatic:

"My old friend here will tell you that I have an impish habit of practical joking. Also that I can never resist a dramatic situation," he tells Lord Cantlemere in "The Mazarin Stone."

"Watson insists that I am the dramatist in real life . . . Some touch of the artist wells up within me and calls insistently for a well-staged performance . . ." (Perhaps a relic of his old acting days?) "Surely our profession . . . would be a drab and sordid one if we did not sometimes set the scene as to glorify our results? The blunt accusation, the brutal tap upon the shoulder—what can one make of such a *dénouement*? But the quick inference, the subtle trap, the clever forecast of coming events, the triumphant vindication of bold theories—are these not the pride and justification of our life's work?" (*The Valley of Fear*)

There are times when both Holmes and Watson speculate on how different things might have been if Holmes had decided to step across to the other side of the line . . .

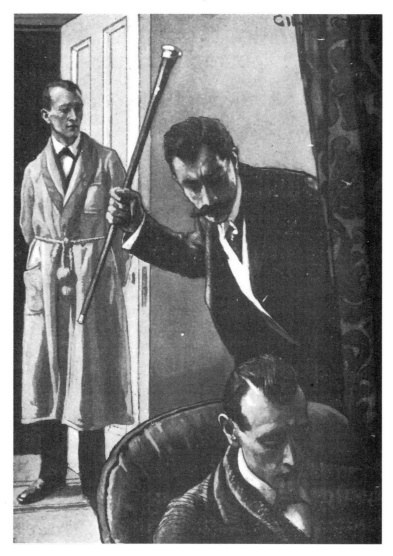

"A cool, sardonic voice greeted him from the open bedroom door: 'Don't break it, Count! Don't break it!'" Holmes and Count Negretto Silvius. (Albert Gilbert for "The Mazarin Stone," 1921)

"So swift, silent, and furtive were his movements, like those of a trained bloodhound picking out a scent, that I could not but think what a terrible criminal he would have made had he turned his energy and sagacity against the law instead of exerting them in its defence," Watson observes in *The Sign of Four*.

"I don't mind confessing to you that I have always had an idea that I would have made a highly efficient criminal." ("Charles Augustus Milverton") "Holmes had remarkable powers, carefully cultivated, of seeing in the dark."

In that same case, he is given the opportunity to try his hand, when he and Watson decide to break into Milverton's house to retrieve some incriminating evidence . . .

"Burglary has always been an alternative profession, had I cared to adopt it, and I have little doubt that I should have come to the front." Nor has Watson, when he sees Holmes in action . . . "I knew that the opening of safes was a particular hobby with him . . . Holmes worked with concentrated energy, laying down one tool, picking up another, handling each with the strength and delicacy of the trained mechanic."

And in another expression of that multi-faceted personality . . .

"Suppose I were any of the fifty men who have good reason for taking my life, how long would I survive against my own pursuit?" ("The Bruce-Partington Plans")

*   *   *   *

Contradiction was fundamental to Holmes's nature . . .

"It has always been my habit to hide none of my methods, either from my friend Watson or from anyone who might take an intelligent interest in them," Holmes declares in "The Reigate Squires." But that was *after* the event.

In Watson's perception, "There was a curious secretive streak in the man which led to many dramatic effects, but left even his closest friend guessing as to what his exact plans might be. He pushed to an extreme the axiom that the only safe plotter was he who plotted alone. I was nearer to him than anyone else, and yet I was always conscious of the gap between." ("The Illustrious Client") "One of Sherlock Holmes's defects—if, indeed, one may call it a defect—was that he was exceedingly loath to communicate his full plans to any other person until the instant of their fulfillment. Partly it came no doubt from his own masterful nature, which loved to dominate and surprise those who were around him. Partly also from his professional caution, which urged him never to take any chances. The result, however, was very trying for those who were acting as his agents and assistants." (*The Hound of the Baskervilles*)

"I do not waste words or disclose my thoughts while a case is actually under consideration." ("The Blanched Soldier") . . . "I am afraid that I rather give myself away when I explain. Results without causes are much more impressive." ("The Stockbroker's Clerk")

As his career developed, Holmes became even more wary about sharing his insights . . .

"I begin to think, Watson, that I make a mistake in explaining. *Omne ignotum pro magnifico*, you know, and my poor little reputation, such as it is, will suffer shipwreck if I am so candid." ("The Red-Headed League") . . . "You know a conjurer gets no credit when once he has explained his trick . . ." (*A Study in Scarlet*)

. . . to the point where he would erect a mental screen of self-defense . . .

"I endeavoured to sound him upon that point but he always glided away to some other topic, until at last I gave over in despair." ("The Blue Carbuncle")

* * * *

Although working relations between Holmes and Watson were generally amenable, there were times when Watson found his friend's behavior less than pleasing.

"I was repelled by the egotism which I had more than once observed to be a strong factor in my friend's singular character" ("The Noble Bachelor") . . . "It was one of the peculiarities of his proud, self-contained nature that though he docketed any fresh information very quietly and accurately in his brain, he seldom made any acknowledgement to the giver." ("The Sussex Vampire")

"I had already observed that he was as sensitive to flattery on the score of his art as any girl could be of her beauty." (*A Study in Scarlet*)

Fortunately, there was a reverse side to the coin. Holmes could also be properly modest . . .

"Holmes was accessible upon the side of flattery, and also, to do him justice, upon the side of kindliness." ("The Retired Colourman")

"A flush of colour sprang to Holmes's pale cheeks, and he bowed to us like the master dramatist who receives the homage of his audience. It was at such moments that for an instant he ceased to be a reasoning machine, and betrayed his human love for admiration and applause. The same singularly proud and reserved nature which turned away with disdain from popular notoriety was capable of being moved to its depths by spontaneous wonder and praise from a friend." ("The Six Napoleons") . . . "He was always warmed by genuine admiration—the characteristic of the real artist." (*The Valley of Fear*)

In fact, Holmes could often be at his most charming at the least likely moments . . .

"He was ready to take that half-comic and wholly philosophic view which was natural to him when his affairs were going awry." ("The Missing Three-Quarter")

"I made a blunder, Watson—which is, I am afraid, a more common occurrence than anyone would think who only knew me through your memoirs." ("The Speckled Band")

. . . and could raise self-deprecation to comic heights . . .

"I think, Watson, that you are now standing in the presence of one of the absolute fools of Europe." ("The Man with the Twisted Lip")

"What a blind beetle I have been not to draw my conclusion!" ("The Noble Bachelor") . . . "I confess I have been as blind as a mole, but it is better to learn wisdom late than never to learn it at all." ("The Man with the Twisted Lip")

He found a perverse pleasure in professional frustration. "There is nothing more stimulating than a case where everything goes against you." (*The Hound of the Baskervilles*)

*   *   *   *

"I play the game for the game's own sake." ("The Bruce-Partington Plans")

Had Holmes taken all the cases that were offered to him over the years, he would undoubtedly have become a very wealthy man. As it was, for the "princely" rent he paid he could certainly have brought the Baker Street premises outright and he appears to have had no difficulty raising the money to buy out Watson's practice (anonymously through a relative) after his return from Reichenbach.

Nor did he need to stint himself when it came to eating out, attending concerts or travelling first class . . . and his cocaine habit cannot have been exactly cheap.

But the fact of the matter was that money was not the object of the Holmes exercise. His own criteria were very different:

"Working as he did rather for the love of his art than for the acquirement of wealth, he refused to associate himself with any investigation which did not tend towards the unusual, and even the fantastic"... "I can assure you, Watson, that the social status of the client is of less moment to me than the interests of his case." ("The Noble Bachelor")

In "A Case of Identity" he talked of having "some ten or twelve" on hand. "They are important, you understand, without being interesting.""A Client is to me a mere unit, a factor in a problem." (*The Sign of Four*) "As to reward, my profession is its own reward; but you are at liberty to defray whatever expenses I may be put to at the time which suits you best." ("The Speckled Band")

"So unworldly was he—or so capricious—that he frequently refused his help to the powerful and wealthy, where the problem made no appeal to his sympathies, while he would devote weeks of most intense application to the affairs of some humble client whose case presented those strange and dramatic qualities which appealed to his imagination and challenged his ingenuity." ("Black Peter")

"'My professional charges are on a fixed scale,' said Holmes coldly. 'I do not vary them, save when I remit them altogether.'" ("Thor Bridge")

There were, of course, occasional exceptions when the payments were "princely." In the matter of "The Priory School" the Duke of Holdernesse was not his favorite client and Holmes was perfectly prepared to take the Duke's money—"Holmes folded up his cheque and placed it carefully in his notebook. 'I am a poor man,' said he, as he patted it affectionately, and thrust it into the depths of his inner pocket." No doubt to be deposited forthwith into the Capital and Counties Bank (Oxford Street branch), where he kept his account, before his benefactor had second thoughts.

Occasionally he would accept a small gift in lieu of a fee. A "snuff-box of old gold with a great amethyst in the centre of the lid" was the reward from the King of Bohemia—although Holmes prized the photograph of Irene Adler infinitely higher . . . the 'brilliant' ring . . . but without doubt he regarded his highest accolade as "a day spent at Windsor," whence he returned with "a remarkably fine emerald tie-pin". . . "a present from a certain gracious lady in whose interests he had once been fortunate enough to carry out a small commission."

Strangely, he steadfastly refused a knighthood—though it was made obvious that it was available on more than one occasion— and yet he accepted the French *Légion d'Honneur*. Whether he realized it or not, the award made him a *Chevalier*, which gave him the right to be called a Knight in England.

* * * *

"Mr. Sherlock Holmes was in active practice for twenty-three years and during seventeen of these I was allowed to co-operate with him and to keep notes of his doings." ("The Veiled Lodger")

Unfortunately, Watson left us details of only some sixty cases— with tantalizing hints of "hundreds to which I have never alluded."

For this we have only Holmes himself to blame. Throughout his career he was at best ambivalent about Watson's attempts to record what he disingenuously referred to as his "trifling experiences." . . . "I have continually been faced by difficulties caused by his own aversion to publicity. To his sombre and cynical spirit all popular applause was always abhorrent . . . it was this attitude upon the part of my friend, and certainly not any lack of interesting material which has caused me of late years to lay very few of my records before the public." ("The Devil's Foot")

However, Watson does allude to a number of other cases, (which, alas, will now remain unchronicled) in his inimitable fashion— "Some, and not the least interesting, were complete failures . . ." And some predated Watson's association with Holmes, so that he could only refer to them at secondhand—such as "the singular tragedy of the Atkinson brothers at Trincomalee" . . . or Holmes's summons to Odessa in the case of the Trepoff murder . . . The Tarlton murders . . . the Tired Captain . . . the case of Vamberry, the wine merchant . . . the singular case of the aluminum crutch . . . of "Ricoletti and his abominable wife." "'These are the records of your early work, then?' I asked. 'I have often wished I had notes of those cases.'

'Yes, my boy; these were all done prematurely, before my biographer had come to glorify me.'" ("The Musgrave Ritual")

Watson says that "Of all the problems which I have been submitted to my friend, Mr. Sherlock Holmes, for solution during the years of our intimacy, there were only two which I was the means of introducing to his notice." One was "The Engineer's Thumb" and the other "that of Colonel Warburton's madness"—of which, alas, we hear nothing further.

One would love to know more, for instance, about the Abernetty Family—a "dreadful business" which Holmes considered to be one of his "classic cases" and one which he solved by observing "the depth (to) which the parsley had sunk into the butter upon a hot day."

. . . the Amateur Mendicant Society, an organization that "held a luxurious club in the lower vault of a furniture warehouse" and that came to Holmes's attention in 1887.

. . . the Camberwell Poisoning Case of the same year, in which "Holmes was able, by winding up the dead man's watch, to prove that it had been wound up two hours ago, and that therefore the deceased had gone to bed within that time—a deduction which was of the greatest importance in clearing up the case." . . .

"The year '87 furnished us with a large series of cases of greater or less interest, of which I retain the records." Among them was the investigation into "the singular adventures of Grice Patersons in the Island of Uffa" . . . not to mention "the adventure of the Paradol Chamber."

The narration of *The Hound of the Baskervilles* (1888) had to wait until Holmes had tidied up two other cases "of the utmost importance . . . in the second he had defended the unfortunate Mme. Montpensier from the charge of murder which hung over her in connection with the death of her step-daughter, Mlle. Carère, the young lady, who, as it will be remembered, was found six months later alive and married in New York." Holmes's initial 'involvement' in the case had been delayed by his prior commitment to the little affair of the Vatican cameos.

The sea was a recurrent theme in many cases. There was the mystery of the cutter *Alicia*, which "sailed one spring morning into a small patch of mist from where she never emerged, nor was anything further ever heard of herself and her crew." Even Holmes never solved that domestic version of the Bermuda Triangle.

. . . another ship, the Dutch steamship, *Friesland*, an affair in which Holmes and Watson nearly lost their lives . . . and the facts concerning the loss of the British barque, *Sophy Anderson*.

. . . and, of course, the *Matilda Briggs*, the ship forever associated with the giant rat of Sumatra, "a story for which the world is not yet prepared"—and now never will be. Can it have been any more horrific, one wonders, than that of Crosby, the banker who met a "terrible death" in 1894, which was somehow connected with "the repulsive story of the red leech"?

One of the many other cases Holmes tackled in that same year of his 'rebirth' was that of "the Addleton tragedy and the singular contents of the ancient British barrow" not to mention "the famous Smith-Mortimer succession case."

And whatever happened to James Phillimore, "who, stepping back into his house to get an umbrella, was never more seen in this world"? . . . or Isadora Persano, the "well-known journalist and duelist, who was found stark staring mad with a match box in front of him which contained a remarkable worm said to be unknown to science"?—a case Holmes dealt with before he met Watson? . . . or Cardinal Tosca, whose sudden death was investigated by Holmes in 1895 "at the express desire of His Holiness the Pope"? . . . or Wilson, "the notorious canary trainer" whose arrest by Holmes in the same year "removed a plague spot from the East End of London"?

In 1898—at the time when he became involved with "The Retired Colourman"—Holmes was "preoccupied with this case of the two Coptic Patriarchs."

Or what about 1901 and the case of the Ferrers documents— not to mention the Abergavenny murder?

But among the more fascinatingly bizarre cases surely there can have been few to rival that of the Dundas separation case in which "the husband was a teetotaller, there was no other woman, and the conduct complained of was that he had drifted into the habit of winding up every meal by taking out his false teeth and hurling them at his wife, which you will allow is not an action likely to occur to the imagination of the average story-teller."

Politics loomed large in many of the cases, such as the case involving the Netherland-Sumatra Company. Since the whole question of how the company was involved "in the colossal schemes of Baron Maupertius," was "too recent in the minds of the public, and . . . too intimately concerned with politics and finance to be fitting subjects for this series of sketches," Watson concluded. Holmes finally brought Maupertius to book in the spring of that hectic 1887 but at considerable cost to himself. "Even (Holmes's) iron constitution . . . had broken down under the strain of an investigation which had extended over two months, during which period he had never worked less than fifteen hours a day and had more than once, as he assured me, kept to his task for five days at a stretch . . . prey to the blackest depression . . . he had succeeded where the police of three countries had failed and out manoeuvered at every point the most accomplished swindler in Europe."

And what was the mysterious link between "the politician, the lighthouse and the trained cormorant" that threatened such a "major scandal" that it stilled Watson's pen? Was it the precursor to the political scandals that have become so prevalent in our jaded times? It is known that "attempts were made to get at and destroy these papers" and that "the source of these outrages" was known, causing Watson to publicly warn that "if they are repeated I have Mr. Holmes's authority for saying that the whole story . . . will be given to the public." Unfortunately for any Holmes biographer, they were not and it was not . . . like so many more.

* * * *

Each case to some degree provided that temporary escape from *ennui* which Holmes craved so badly and when Watson heard— "This is certainly very singular"—he must have breathed a sigh of relief to know that another game would soon be afoot. And if that was followed by—"These are very deep waters"—then it was likely to be a game worth playing.

But once the game was over and he heard—"The case has, in some respect, been not entirely devoid of interest"—then he waited to see the brightness fade from the eye and the alertness from the body language, as his friend retreated to the state he believed to be permanent throughout his career, that self-fulfilling prophecy Watson knew it was his duty to try and keep at bay . . .

"What is the use of having powers . . . when one has no field upon which to exert them? Crime is commonplace, existence is commonplace, and no qualities save those which are commonplace have any function upon earth." (*The Sign of Four*) ". . . the days of the great cases are past. Man, or at least criminal man, has lost all enterprise and originality. As to my own little practice, it seems to be degenerating into an agency for recovering lost lead pencils and giving advice to young ladies from boarding-schools." ("The Copper Beeches")

*   *   *   *

It is estimated that by the time he retired in 1903 Sherlock Holmes had been involved in approximately 1,700 cases. Of the sixty cases recorded by Dr. Watson, fifteen involved no crime at all. There were only eight cases involving murder.

"It's every man's business to see justice done." ("The Crooked Man")

"Here Are the Regulars"

"Here are the regulars; so the auxiliary forces may beat a retreat."

—The Sign of Four

"I am not retained by the police to supply their deficiencies."

—"The Blue Carbuncle"

"I am the last and highest court of appeal in detection. When Gregson, or Lestrade, or Athelney Jones are out of their depths—which, by the way, is their normal state—the matter is laid before me. I examine the data, as an expert, and pronounce a specialist's opinion. I claim no credit in such cases. The work itself, the pleasure of finding a field for my peculiar powers, is my highest reward."

—The Sign of Four

* * * *

H OLMES'S RELATIONS with the 'regulars' of the London Metropolitan Police at Scotland Yard would ebb and flow during the twenty-three years that he was in practice. Invariably some official nose or other would be out of joint and there was always a strong element of competition in any given case, but over the years a degree of accommodation was reached. And when a particularly perplexing case turned up, it was invariably to Baker Street—eagerly or reluctantly—that the regulars would turn for advice.

Holmes, for his part, insisted repeatedly that he was not out to steal their glory and would periodically list the cases that he had been instrumental in solving where he had allowed them to take sole credit. "You may look upon me simply as an irregular pioneer who goes in front of the regular force of the country." ("The Missing Three-Quarter") When Forbes, the official attempting to retrieve the missing Naval Treaty, accuses him: "You are ready enough to use all the information that the police can lay at your disposal, and then you try to finish the case yourself and bring discredit on them," Holmes rebukes him with—"On the contrary, out of my last fifty-three cases my name has only appeared in four, and the police have had all the credit in forty-nine. I don't blame you for not knowing this, for you are young and inexperienced, but if you wish to get on in your new duties you will work with me and not against me."

In "The Retired Colourman" another "smart young police Inspector"—MacKinnon—has clearly learned the lesson well—"That is very handsome of you, Mr. Holmes. Praise or blame can matter little to you, but it is very different to us when the newspapers begin to ask questions." No wonder Holmes considered him "a good fellow."

The London force was called 'Scotland Yard' in popular parlance after its location on the Thames Embankment. In fact, it had two embodiments in Holmes's time. The original structure, Great Scotland Yard, was virtually destroyed in a terrorist bombing in May 1884, and the complex that eventually replaced it in 1890 was technically New Scotland Yard. The events of 1884, caused by the Fenian movement—which also included the blowing up of the Metropolitan Railway—prompted the setting up of Scotland Yard's 'Special Branch' or Criminal Investigation Department (CID) and it was with them that Holmes and Watson were most often involved.

* * * *

"I have been down to see friend Lestrade at the Yard. There may be an occasional want of imaginative intuition down there, but they lead the world for thoroughness and method." ("The Three Garridebs")

Primus inter pares of the Scotland Yard officers was undoubtedly Inspector (George?) Lestrade, a long-serving officer. During the 1880s it was claimed that he already had twenty years' service under his belt.

Lestrade was on duty during the first adventure Holmes and Watson shared, *A Study in Scarlet* in 1881. Watson described him as "lean and ferret-like . . . a little sallow, rat-faced, dark-eyed fellow." However, in the same narrative he refers to Lestrade's "bulldog features." A rat-faced bulldog would surely have struck terror into the hearts of Victorian evildoers.

Holmes has no great regard for Lestrade's mental acuity and in "The Boscombe Valley Mystery" is sufficiently irritated with the detective's obtuseness to refer to him as "that imbecile Lestrade" but in *The Hound of the Baskervilles*—another case in which Lestrade became latterly involved—he does admit that that "small, wiry bulldog of a man" is "the best of the professionals." A year later—during the case of "The Cardboard Box"—Lestrade is "wiry, as dapper and as ferret-like as ever" and in Holmes's current estimation—"although he is absolutely devoid of reason, he is as

"We all three [Lestrade, Holmes, and Watson] shook hands." (Sidney Paget for *The Hound of the Baskervilles*, 1902)

tenacious as a bulldog when he once understands what he has to do, and indeed, it is just this tenacity which has brought him to the top at Scotland Yard." Throughout their association his main complaint about the Inspector was that "You do not add imagination to your other qualities."

Over the years their professional relationship distinctly evolved. In *A Study in Scarlet* the Inspector is overly dismissive— "You may be smart and clever, but the old hound is the best, when all is said and done." In "The Noble Bachelor" Lestrade is critical of what he perceives to be Holmes's dilettante ways—"I believe in hard work, and not in sitting by the fire spinning fine theories.""I am a practical man, Mr. Holmes, and when I have got my evidence I come to my conclusions." ("The Norwood Builder") Even though he will soon be a regular visitor to that particular fireside to hear a few of those theories. "It was no very unusual thing for (him) to look in upon us of an evening and his visits were welcome to Sherlock Holmes, for they enabled him to keep in touch with what was going on at the police headquarters." ("The Six Napoleons")

"Good afternoon, Lestrade! You will find an extra tumbler upon the sideboard, and there are cigars in the box." ("The Noble Bachelor")

In "The Six Napoleons" Lestrade seems to be about to give Holmes a lesson in the principles of detection—"You are aware that no two thumb-marks are alike?"—but then thinks better of it. Or are we witnessing a rare spark of Lestrade humor? In point of fact, Lestrade was ahead of his time. Scotland Yard did not adopt the Galton fingerprint test until 1901.

Over time Lestrade appreciated what he had in Holmes and was big enough to admit, "You are too many for me when you begin to get on your theories" and even by the end of "The Noble Bachelor"—"it is difficult for me to refuse you anything, for you have

"Holmes smiled and clapped Lestrade on the shoulder." (Sidney Paget for "The Norwood Builder," 1903)

been of use to the force once or twice in the past, and we owe you a good turn at Scotland Yard."

In a strange way Holmes came to regard him as something of a *protégé*, for when he first encounters Lestrade after returning from the Great Hiatus in 1894, he chides the Inspector for having failed to solve three murders in one year, although he was successful in the case of "The Molesey Mystery," telling him, "you handled it fairly well."

After "The Six Napoleons" (1900) Lestrade is positively effusive in his thanks. "We're not jealous of you at Scotland Yard. No, sir, we are very proud of you, and if you come down tomorrow, there's not a man, from the oldest Inspector to the youngest constable, who wouldn't be glad to shake you by the hand."

"'Thank you!' said Holmes. 'Thank you!' and as he turned away it seemed to me that he was more nearly moved by the softer human emotions than I had ever seen him."

* * * *

A close second to Lestrade was Inspector Tobias Gregson. In *A Study in Scarlet* Holmes told Watson—"Gregson is the smartest of the Scotland Yarders; he and Lestrade are the pick of a bad lot. They are both quick and energetic, but conventional—shockingly so. They have their knives into one another, too. They are as jealous as a pair of professional beauties." If they did, it never became really apparent in Watson's narratives and their professional paths rarely crossed.

Holmes also added in "The Red Circle" that "Our official detectives may blunder in the matter of intelligence, but never in that of courage."

When we meet Gregson in *A Study in Scarlet*, Watson describes him as "a tall, white-faced, flaxen-haired man, with a notebook in his

Lestrade points out the puzzling RACHE to Watson, Holmes, and Inspector
Gregson. (D. H. Friston for A *Study in Scarlet*, 1887)

hand" and by the time of "Wisteria Lodge" (1890) he describes him as "an energetic, gallant, and within his limitations, a capable officer." "Were he but gifted with imagination, he might rise to great heights in his profession." ("The Speckled Band")

He was known to have worked with Holmes and Watson on *A Study in Scarlet, The Sign of Four,* "The Greek Interpreter," "The Red Circle" and "Wisteria Lodge." ("He knows that I (Holmes) am his superior, and acknowledges it to me; but he would cut his tongue out before he would own it to any third person.")

*   *   *   *

In charge of the investigation in *The Sign of Four* was Inspector Athelney Jones . . . "a very stout, portly man . . . red-faced, burly and plethoric with a pair of very small, twinkling eyes, which looked keenly out from between swollen and puffy pouches." Holmes grudgingly admitted that "he has occasional glimmerings of reason."

At the *dénouement* of "The Red-Headed League" Holmes calls in Inspector Peter Jones. "I thought it well to have Jones with us also, he is not a bad fellow, though an absolute imbecile in his profession. He has one positive virtue. He is brave as a bulldog, and tenacious as a lobster if he gets his claws upon anyone." Holmes's sourness may well have been conditioned by hearing Jones's patronizing view of his own prowess—"Your friend, Mr. Sherlock Holmes, is a wonderful man, sir. He's a man who is not to be beat. I have known that young man go into a good many cases, but I never saw the case yet that he could not throw a light upon . . ." (*The Sign of Four*) "You may place considerable confidence in Mr. Holmes, sir. He has his own little methods, which are . . . just a little too theoretical and fantastic but he has the makings of a detective in him."

Much more to Holmes's taste was Inspector Alec MacDonald, who assisted in *The Valley of Fear*. "He was a young but trusted member of the detective force who had distinguished himself in several cases which had been entrusted to him," Watson wrote—"His tall, bony figure gave promise of exceptional physical strength, while his great cranium and deep-set lustrous eyes spoke no less clearly of the keen intelligence which twinkled out from behind his bushy eyebrows. He was a silent, precise man, with a dour nature and a hard Aberdonian accent . . . Holmes was not prone to friendship but he was tolerant of the big Scotchman."

But of the younger generation Holmes's favorite for a while seemed to be Inspector Stanley Hopkins, "a promising detective, in whose career Holmes had several times shown a very practical interest." "An exceedingly alert man, thirty years of age, dressed in a quiet tweed suit but retaining the erect bearing of one who was accustomed to official uniform." ("Black Peter" 1895) In that case Hopkins "professed the admiration and respect of a pupil for the scientific methods of the famous amateur" and Holmes—who was not averse to flattery—later told Watson ("The Abbey Grange" 1897), "Hopkins has called me in seven times, and on each occasion his summons has been entirely justified . . . I fancy that every one of his cases has found its way into your collection."

However, even Hopkins was not always to be spared his teacher's tongue. In "The Golden Pince-Nez" Holmes asks him—"What did you do, Hopkins, after you had made certain that you had made certain of nothing?"—and his final verdict was "I am disappointed in Stanley Hopkins. I had hoped for better things from him."

Among the supporting cast from Scotland Yard were Inspector Bradstreet (who was on hand for "The Man with the Twisted Lip," "The Blue Carbuncle" and "The Engineer's

"Leaning forward in the car, Holmes listened intently to MacDonald's short sketch of the problem which awaited us in Sussex." (Frank Wiles for *The Valley of Fear*, 1914)

Thumb") . . . Inspector Forrester, "a smart young fellow" in "The Reigate Squires" . . . Inspector Morton, an old acquaintance of Holmes, who turned up in "The Dying Detective" "dressed up in unofficial tweeds" . . . and the off-stage Inspector Patterson, who was left to tidy up the Moriarty gang after Holmes and Watson's departure.

Ironically, the police officer for whom Holmes was to have the highest regard was not employed by Scotland Yard but by a provincial force.

Holmes encountered Inspector Baynes of the Surrey constabulary during the adventure of "Wisteria Lodge." He "was a stout, puffy, red man, whose face was only redeemed from grossness by two extraordinary bright eyes, almost hidden behind the heavy creases of cheek and brow." Working independently of Holmes and Watson, Baynes earned at least a draw in solving the case. Possibly almost as satisfying to Baynes was Holmes's "Your powers, if I may say so without offence, seem superior to your opportunities . . . You will rise high in your profession. You have instinct and intuition."

＊　＊　＊　＊

"I go into a case to help the ends of justice and the work of the police. If ever I have separated myself from the official force, it is because they have first separated themselves from me. I have no wish ever to score at their expense." (*The Valley of Fear*)

There were, needless to say, many occasions when that separation took place and Holmes and Watson were left to their own devices. At which point . . . "I shall be my own police. When I have spun my web they may take the flies." ("The Five Orange Pips")

In spinning his own web Holmes had a number of resources that he employed from time to time. There was Toby, the talented

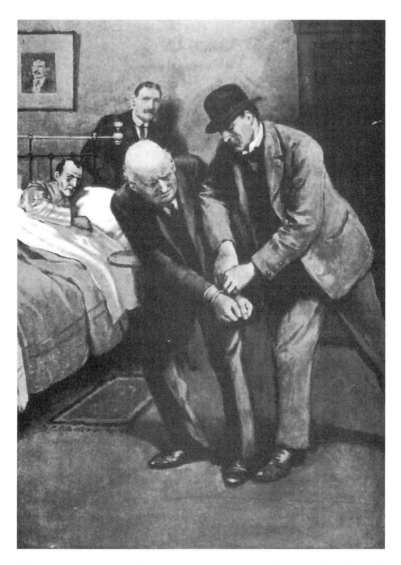

"'You'll only get yourself hurt,' said the Inspector. 'Stand still, will you?'"
Inspector Morton apprehends Culverton Smith. (Walter Paget for "The
Dying Detective," 1914)

hound belonging to the taxidermist, 'Old Sherman of Lambeth,' which helped Holmes solve a key problem in *The Sign of Four*. Watson was sent to collect Toby and found "a queer mongrel with a most amazing power of scent . . . an ugly, long-haired, lop-eared creature, half spaniel and half lurcher, brown and white in colour, with a very clumsy, waddling gait." But Holmes was emphatic that "I would rather have Toby's help than that of the whole detective force of London."

Running Toby a close second was Pompey, "a detective who was very eminent in the art of tracking." Pompey was "a squat, lop-eared, white-and-tan dog, something between a beagle and a fox-hound . . . no great flier, as his build showed, but a staunch hound on a scent." He helped Holmes to locate the "Missing Three-Quarter."

"Dogs don't make mistakes." ("Shoscombe Old Place")

And then there were The Baker Street Irregulars, ("the Baker Street division of the detective police force," as Holmes called them.) . . .

The Irregulars were a gang of street urchins recruited by Holmes to perform a variety of tasks, such as pursuing leads in areas where Holmes himself could not go without being noticed. Watson first met them in *A Study in Scarlet*—"six dirty little scoundrels (who) stood in line like so many disreputable statuettes." Their leader at the time was one Wiggins.

"One of their number, taller and older than the others, stood forward with an air of lounging superiority which was very funny in such a disreputable little scarecrow."

Holmes claimed—"There's more work to be got out of one of those little beggars than out of a dozen of the force . . . The mere sight of an official looking person seals men's lips. These youngsters, however, can go everywhere, see everything, overhear everyone. They are as sharp as needles, too; all they want is organisation."

Sherlock Holmes and Pompey. (Frederic Dorr Steele for "The Missing Three-Quarter," 1904)

Over the years, naturally, the members of the group came and went or (literally) outgrew the job, but it was one that was valued highly. Holmes paid each of them a shilling a day when they were on a job, while the boy who found the object of their search was given a bonus of a guinea—a small fortune for those days.

In the early 1900s—when Watson had finally moved out of Baker Street—Holmes took on other occasional helpers and set up a "small, but very efficient organisation," which he occasionally referred to as an 'Agency.'

There was Mercer, "a general utility man who looks up routine business" . . . and Langdale Pike, "a human book of reference upon all matters of scandal." In "The Three Gables" Watson described him as "This strange languid creature (who) spent his waking hours in the bow-window of a St. James Street club (probably Boodles at No. 28) and was the receiving station as well as the transmitter for all gossip in the metropolis. He made, it was said, a four-figure income by the paragraphs he contributed every week to the garbage papers which cater to the inquisitive public. If ever, far down in the turbid depths of London life, there was some strange swirl or eddy, it was marked with automatic exactness by this human dial above the surface. Holmes discreetly helped Langdale to knowledge and on occasion was helped in turn." A founder member of today's gossip column fraternity . . .

There was the mysterious 'Fred Porlock' . . . "'Porlock, Watson, is a *nom de plume,* a mere identification, but behind it lies a shifty and evasive personality. In a former letter he frankly informed me that the name was not his own, and defied me ever to trace him among the teeming millions of this great city. Porlock is important, not for himself, but for the great man with whom he is in touch (Moriarty) . . . Led on by some rudimentary aspirations towards right, and encouraged by the judicious stimulation of an occasional ten-pound note sent to him by devious methods, he has once or twice given me advance information which has been of value—the highest value which anticipates and prevents rather than avenges crime."

Was the "shifty and evasive personality," this Victorian 'Deep Throat,' "a student of Coleridge," one wonders? Was it not "the person on business from Porlock" who disturbed the poet when he was in full flow with—in Xanadu did Kubla Khan/A stately pleasure-dome decree?

There was also the unlikely figure of Shinwell Johnson (a.k.a. Porky Shinwell) . . . "a huge, coarse, red-faced, scorbutic man with a pair of vivid black eyes which were the only external sign of the cunning mind within." Johnson was on hand in the case of "The Illustrious Client." He was not at all Watson's idea of a suitable *confrère*—"Johnson, I grieve to say, made his name first as a very dangerous villain and served two terms at Parkhurst. Finally he repented and allied himself to Holmes, acting as his agent in the huge criminal underground of London and obtaining information which proved to be of vital importance . . . with the glamour of his two convictions upon him, he had the *entrée* of every night club, doss house and gambling den in the town."

*   *   *   *

Not surprisingly, Holmes's reputation became worldwide and he was able to create an informal network of overseas contacts, which proved useful from time to time—most particularly in the Continental cases that Watson often alludes to but rarely describes in detail—the case involving the Dutch royal family in 1881 ("the matter in which I served them was of such delicacy that I cannot confide it even to you, (Watson) who have been good enough to chronicle one or two of my little problems."); the "service to the royal family of Scandinavia" in 1890; the "matter of supreme importance to the French government" in 1891; and the affair of Huret, "'The Boulevard Assassin' in 1894, an exploit which won for Holmes an autograph letter of thanks from the French President and the Order of the Legion of Honour."

Somewhere during his Gaelic involvement Holmes made the professional acquaintance of Francois le Villard, a French detective. The admiration was mutual. Holmes told Watson that Villard had "all the Celtic power of quick intuition; but he is deficient in the wide range of exact knowledge which is essential to the higher developments of his art . . . He possesses two out of the three qualities necessary for the ideal detective. He has the power of observation and that of deduction. He is only wanting in knowledge and that may come in time." Villard also translated some of Holmes's monographs into French.

Much less impressive to Holmes was Edgar Allan Poe's (1809–1849) detective, C. Auguste Dupin, hero of such works as *The Murders in the Rue Morgue* (1841) and *The Purloined Letter* (1845). In *A Study in Scarlet* Holmes was distinctly unflattered to be compared by Watson to that "fictional" detective.

"No doubt you think you are complimenting me in comparing me to Dupin . . . now, in my opinion, Dupin was a very inferior fellow. That trick of his of breaking in on his friend's thoughts with an apropos remark after a quarter of an hour's silence is really very showy and superficial. He had some analytical genius, no doubt, but he was by no means such a phenomenon as Poe appeared to imagine."

Since Holmes himself has been known to utilize a very similar technique to create dramatic surprise, there would seem to be the slightest hint of sour grapes in the air.

And when Watson asks him if he has read the works of Emile Gaboriau (1832–1873), pioneer of the *romans policiers*, "Does

Lecoq come up to your idea of a detective?"—Holmes is even more dismissive:

"Lecoq was a miserable bungler. He had only one thing to recommend him, and that was his energy. That book made me positively ill. The question was how to identify an unknown prisoner. I could have done it in twenty-four hours. Lecoq took six months or so. It might be made a text-book for detectives to teach them what to avoid." (*A Study in Scarlet*)

That Holmes's vanity could be scratched closer to home was indicated again towards the end of his career. His success as a private investigator had, not surprisingly, brought forth numerous inferior copyists. In all of Watson's accounts only one is thought worthy of mention—when in the case of "The Retired Colourman," Holmes refers to "Barker, my hated rival on the Surrey shore . . . a tall, dark man . . . He has several good cases to his credit . . . his methods are irregular, no doubt like my own." Watson describes him as "heavily-moustached, rather military-looking man . . . with tinted glasses." It would have been fascinating to know what the man had done to attract both the notice and the comment.

*   *   *   *

Holmes's presence and achievements on the London scene encouraged significant changes in police procedure.

When he and Watson first meet, he has at that very moment perfected a test to determine beyond doubt the presence of blood stains at the scene of a crime. There were other innovations— many of them initially belittled by the official force—that were slowly but surely to be adopted and made part of their thinking.

"Since I ran down that coiner by the zinc and copper filings in the seam of his cuff, they have begun to realise the importance of the microscope." ("Shoscombe Old Place")

Over the years the force—unwittingly or not—got into Holmes's habit of leaving the crime scene untouched until it could be examined by experts, and paying due attention to footprints, even going so far as to copy his practice of making plaster casts for later matching.

The force certainly had their own system of filing information on known criminals and patterns of criminal behavior but Holmes's careful indexing and codifying undoubtedly encouraged them to set up the Criminal Records Office.

They even took to emulating his technique of trying to think with the criminal's mind . . . "You'll get results . . . by always putting yourself in the other fellow's place, and thinking what you would do yourself. It takes some imagination but it pays."

Holmes made it his business to keep *au fait* with the relevant work of others. In "The Naval Treaty" he expresses his admiration for the Frenchman, Alphonse Bertillon (1853–1914), whose system, the Bertillonage, used a complex method of body measurements, together with detailed files and photographs, to aid in the identification of criminals. Scotland Yard finally adopted Bertillon's system in 1888—only to be overtaken by Sir Francis Galton's method of classifying fingerprints in 1901.

There is an amusing moment in this connection in *The Hound of the Baskervilles* when Dr. Mortimer—visiting Baker Street to apprise Holmes of the Baskerville problem—thinks he is praising Holmes by likening his achievements to those of Bertillon—but giving him *second* place!

"'Recognising, as I do, that you are the second highest expert in Europe—'

'Indeed sir! May I enquire who has the honour to be the first?' asked Holmes with some asperity.

'To the man of precisely scientific mind the work of Monsieur Bertillon must always appeal strongly.'

'Then had you better not consult him?'"

However, in retrospect Holmes would probably have considered his own mark was made more permanent where it counted by the fact that Scotland Yard has now named its main computer system—HOLMES (Home Office Large Major Enquiry Service).

* * * *

While Holmes regarded it as his 'mission'—and what a sardonic smile that word would have elicited—to "help the ends of justice" within the current law, he reserved the right to redefine the law and "justice" on occasion . . .

"Once or twice in my career I feel I have done more real harm by my discovery of the criminal than ever he had done by his crime. I have learned caution now, and I had rather play tricks with the law of England than with my own conscience." ("The Abbey Grange")

On those occasions he effectively *became* the law of England. In "The Abbey Grange," having unmasked Captain Croker he declared himself the ultimate authority . . .

"See here, Captain Croker, we'll do this in due form of law. You are the prisoner. Watson, you are a British jury, and I never met a man who was more eminently fitted to represent one. I am the judge. Now, gentlemen of the jury, you have heard the evidence.

'Not guilty, my lord.' said I.

'*Vox populi, vox Dei*. You are acquitted, Captain Croker. So long as the law does not find some other victim, you are safe from me.'"

"I suppose I shall have to compound a felony as usual." ("The Three Garridebs")

But society had little to fear as far as the real meaning of justice was concerned, as long as the light burned at 221b Baker Street.

*   *   *   *

"On general principles it is best that I should not leave the country. Scotland Yard feels lonely without me, and it causes an unhealthy excitement among the criminal classes." ("The Disappearance of Lady Frances Carfax")

The Napoleons of Crime

O
F ALL THE VILLAINS who crossed Holmes's path during the twenty or so years he was in active practice a handful stand out.

There was the terrifying Dr. Grimesby Roylott of Stoke Moran—particularly distressing to Watson, since the man had at one time also served as a doctor in India. "A large face, seared with a thousand wrinkles, burned yellow with the sun, and marked with every evil passion, was turned from one to the other of us, while his deep-set, bile-shot eyes, and his high, thin, fleshless nose, gave him somewhat the resemblance of a fierce old bird of prey."

In "The Speckled Band" Roylott murders one of his stepdaughters for her inheritance and is about to murder the second, when Holmes and Watson intervene by turning his devilish plan onto its instigator.

Roylott provokes one of Holmes's rare physical exertions. Visiting their consulting rooms he attempts to frighten Holmes by demonstrating his own strength:

"He stepped swiftly forward, seized the poker, and bent it into a curve with his huge brown hands.

'See that you keep yourself out of my grip,' he snarled, and hurling the twisted poker into the fireplace, he strode out of the room.

'He seems a very amiable person,' said Holmes, laughing. 'I am not quite so bulky, but if he had remained I might have shown him that my grip was not much more feeble than his own.' As he spoke he picked up the steel poker, and with a sudden effort straightened it out again."

Then—in "The Red-Headed League"—there was John Clay, "murderer, thief, smasher, and forger . . . a young man but at the head of his profession," of whom one would like to have heard more. Holmes considered him "the fourth smartest man in London and for daring I am not sure that he has not a claim to be third."

Inspector Peter Jones said of Clay—"I would rather have my bracelets on him than on any criminal in London. He's a remarkable man . . . his grandfather was a Royal Duke, and he himself has been to Eton and Oxford. His brain is as cunning as his fingers, and though we meet signs of him at every turn, we never know where to find the man himself. He'll crack a crib in Scotland one week, and be raising money to build an orphanage in Cornwall the next. I've been on his track for years, and have never set eyes on him yet."

Clay was "small, stout-built, very quick in his ways, no hair on his face, though he's not short of thirty. Has a white splash of acid on his forehead." His ears were pierced for earrings. The moment Jabez Wilson described his assistant, 'Vincent Spaulding,' Holmes knew precisely whom he was dealing with.

*   *   *   *

"I tell you, Watson, this time we have a foeman who is worthy of our mettle."

"Which of you is Holmes?" Dr. Grimesby Roylott. (Sidney Paget for "The Speckled Band," 1892)

"It's no use, John Clay." Holmes captures "the fourth smartest man in London, and for daring I am not sure that he has not a claim to be third." (Sidney Paget for "The Red-Headed League," 1891)

Holmes might well have been referring to John Clay but, in fact, the worthy foeman was the subtle Jack Stapleton of *The Hound of the Baskervilles.*

Stapleton posed as a mild-mannered entomologist. Watson meets "a small, slim, clean-shaven, prim-faced man, flaxen-haired and lean-jawed, between thirty and forty years of age, dressed in a grey suit and wearing a straw hat. A tin box for botanical specimens hung over his shoulder, and he carried a green butterfly-net in one of his hands." . . . "His grey clothes and jerky, zig zag, irregular progress made him not unlike some huge moth himself."

Appearances are deceptive, though. In reality, he was a distant relation of Sir Henry Baskerville, whose title he was determined to assume. The resurrection of the legendary and ghostly 'Hound' was his intended means.

Holmes finally comes to the truth by examining the portrait gallery in Baskerville Hall. Looking at a painting of a bewigged Baskerville from the Cavalier period . . .

"He stood upon a chair, and holding up the light in his left hand, he curved his right arm over the broad hat, and round the long ringlets.

'Good heavens!' I cried, in amazement.

The face of Stapleton had sprung out of the canvas.

'Ha, you see it now. My eyes have been trained to examine faces and not their trimmings.'"

"I said it in London, Watson, and I say it again now, that never yet have we helped to hunt down a more dangerous man."

* * * *

Holmes had to deal with more than his fair share of blackmailers.

There was Charles Augustus Milverton in the case of that name. Holmes considered him at the time (1899) to be "the worst man in London.""'I've had to do with fifty murderers in my career but the worst of them never gave me the repulsion which I have for this fellow . . . the king of all the blackmailers" . . . "I had seldom heard my friend speak with such intensity of feeling."

Milverton was "a man of fifty, with a large, intellectual head, a round, plump, hairless face, a perpetual frozen smile, and two keen grey eyes, which gleamed brightly from behind broad, gold-rimmed glasses. Something of Mr. Pickwick's benevolence in his appearance, marred only by the insincerity of the fixed smile and by the hard glitter of those restless and penetrating eyes. His voice was as smooth and suave as his countenance."

"Do you feel a creeping, sinking sensation, Watson, when you stand before the serpents in the Zoo, and see the slithery, gliding, venomous creatures, with their deadly eyes and their wicked, flattened faces? Well, that's how Milverton impresses me."

Holmes and Watson decide on a little burglary to help their client—only to witness Milverton's murder at the hands of another victim. When approached by Lestrade to help with the crime, Holmes for once refuses:

"'I am afraid I can't help you, Lestrade,' said Holmes. 'The fact is that I knew this fellow Milverton, and I considered him one of the most dangerous men in London, and that I think there are certain crimes which the law cannot touch, and which, therefore, to some extent, justify private revenge . . . My sympathies are with the criminals rather than with the victim, and I will not handle this case.'"

*   *   *   *

"There is no more dangerous man in Europe (I have had several opponents to whom that flattering term has been applied)" than Baron Adelbert Gruner, "the Austrian murderer."

Charles Augustus Milverton. (Sidney Paget for "Charles Augustus Milverton," 1904)

Gruner had killed his wife and eliminated the witness to his crime. Now he had ensnared the naïve but stubborn heiress, Violet de Merville, and Holmes had been hired by "The Illustrious Client" (the future King Edward VII) to end the liaison.

"It is my business to follow the details of Continental crime . . . He is said to have the whole sex at his mercy and to have made ample use of the fact . . . A complex mind. All great criminals have that . . . an excellent antagonist, cool as ice, silky voiced and soothing as one of your fashionable consultants and poisonous as a cobra. He has breeding in him—a real aristocrat of crime, with a superficial suggestion of afternoon tea and all the cruelty of the grave behind it."

Watson is sent to meet the Baron.

"He was certainly a remarkably handsome man. His European reputation for beauty was fully deserved. In figure he was not more than of middle size, but was built upon graceful and active lines. His face was swarthy, almost Oriental, with large, dark, languorous eyes which might easily hold an irresistible fascination for women. His hair and moustache were raven black; the latter short, pointed and carefully waxed. His features were regular and pleasing, save only his straight, thin-lipped mouth. If ever I saw a murderer's mouth it was there—a cruel, hard gash in the face, compressed, inexorable, and terrible. He was ill-advised to train his moustache away from it, for it was Nature's danger-signal . . . In age I should have put him at little over thirty, though his record afterwards showed that he was forty-two."

Holmes's problem is solved for him when one of the Baron's discarded mistresses, Kitty Winter, rearranges those 'regular' features with acid.

Potentially lethal was 'Killer' Evans (a.k.a. Morecroft) whose real name was James Winter. An American with an extensive record in the files of Scotland Yard . . .

"Very fine—very fine indeed! Would it be indiscreet if I were to ask you how you obtained it?" Watson and Baron Adelbert Gruner. (Howard Elcock for "The Illustrious Client," 1925)

"Aged forty-four. Native of Chicago. Known to have shot three men in the States. Escaped from penitentiary through political influence. Came to London in 1893. Shot a man over cards in a night-club in the Waterloo Road in January 1895. Man died, but he was shown to have been the aggressor in the row. Dead man was identified as Rodger Prescott, famous as forger and coiner in Chicago. Killer Evans released in 1901. He has been under police supervision since, but so far as known had led an honest life."

Unfortunately, Evans reverted to type when he set up the confidence trick in the affair of "The Three Garridebs"—an affair in which Evans shot Watson and was almost killed by Holmes in retaliation. It was the closest call the two friends ever had.

The rest of the list were strictly supporting actors but, even so, many of them sounded sufficiently interesting that one would have liked to know more—particularly one of Moriarty's men— "Parker . . . a harmless enough fellow . . . a garroter by trade, and a remarkable performer on the Jew's harp."

$*$ $*$ $*$ $*$

"The second most dangerous man in London," according to Holmes was Colonel Sebastian Moran.

When Holmes returns from the Great Hiatus in April 1894 he knows he is being pursued by Moran. By way of briefing Watson, Holmes looks up the entry on the man in his commonplace book:

"'My collection of M's is a fine one . . . here is Morgan the poisoner, and Merridew of abominable memory, and Matthews, who knocked out my left canine in the waiting-room at Charing Cross, and, finally, here is our friend of tonight.' He handed over the book, and I read:

MORAN, Sebastian, Colonel. Unemployed. Formerly Ist Bangalore Pioneers. Born London, 1840. Son of Sir Augustus Moran, C.B., once British Minister to Persia. Educated Eton and Oxford. Served in Jowaki Campaign, Afghanistan Campaign, Charasaib (despatches), Sherpur, and Cabul. Author of *Heavy Game of the Western Himalayas* (1881); *Three Months in the Jungle* (1884). Address: Conduit Street. Clubs: The Anglo-Indian, the Tankerville, The Bagatelle Card Club.

'This is astonishing,' said I, as I handed back the volume. 'The man's career is that of an honourable soldier.'"

Holmes admits that "Up to a certain point he did well. He was always a man of iron nerve . . . (But) there are some trees, Watson, which grow to a certain height, and then suddenly develop some unsightly eccentricity. You will see it often in humans . . . Whatever the cause, Colonel Moran began to go wrong."

At some point he was recruited by Professor Moriarty, "to whom for a time he was chief of staff. Moriarty supplied him liberally with money, and used him only in one or two high-class jobs, which no ordinary criminal could have undertaken . . . So cleverly was the colonel concealed that, even when the Moriarty gang was broken up, we would not incriminate him."

Moran was paid £6,000 a year. "That's paying for brains, you see—the American business principle . . . It's more than the Prime Minister gets."

Earlier—in *The Valley of Fear*—he described Moran as "aloof and guarded and inaccessible to the law . . . the first link in (Moriarty's) chain."

Moran had accompanied Moriarty to the assignation with Holmes at the Reichenbach Falls and was the only one to realize that their dreaded adversary had survived. After Moriarty plunged to his death, it was Moran who fired at Holmes and gave him "an evil five minutes upon the Reichenbach ledge."

Now "the most cunning and dangerous criminal in London," he waited for the detective to reappear and, when he did so, planned to assassinate him with an air rifle from "The Empty House" opposite. Holmes, of course, prevailed and Moran was duly arrested and charged with a previous murder but somehow avoided the death sentence. In "His Last Bow" it is reported that he was still languishing in prison in 1914.

As the blow finally fell . . .

"His two eyes shone like stars and his features were working convulsively. He was an elderly man, with a thin, projecting nose, a high, bald forehead and a huge grizzled moustache . . . His face was gaunt and swarthy, scored with deep, savage lines . . . It was a tremendously virile and yet sinister face . . . with the brow of a philosopher above and the jaw of a sensualist below, the man must have started with great capacities for good or for evil. But one could not look upon his cruel blue eyes, with their drooping, cynical lids, or upon the fierce, aggressive nose and the threatening deep-lined brow without reading Nature's plainest danger-signals. He took no heed of any of us, but his eyes were fixed upon Holmes's face with an expression in which hatred and amazement were equally blended. 'You fiend!' he kept on muttering—'you clever, clever fiend!'"

A sentiment many another of Holmes's opponents would have echoed.

*   *   *   *

And then there was Professor James Moriarty, "the Napoleon of Crime."

"You can tell an old master by the sweep of his brush. I can tell a Moriarty when I see one." (*The Valley of Fear*)

Without doubt Moriarty was the most formidable of Holmes's many adversaries. "He is the Napoleon of Crime, Watson.

"Colonel Moran sprang forward with a snarl of rage." Colonel Sebastian
Moran, "the second most dangerous man in London." (Sidney Paget for
"The Empty House," 1903)

"Professor Moriarty stood before me." (Sidney Paget for "The Final Problem," 1893)

He is the organiser of half that is evil and nearly all that is undetected in this great city. He is a genius, a philosopher, an abstract thinker. He has a brain of the first order. He sits motionless like a spider in the centre of its web, but that web has a thousand radiations, and he knows every quiver of each of them.'" "Petty thefts, wanton assaults, purposeless outrage—to the man who held the clue all could be worked into one connected whole."

"In calling Moriarty a criminal you are uttering a libel in the eyes of the law, and there lies the glory and the wonder of it. The greatest schemer of all time, the organiser of every devilry, the controlling brain of the underworld . . . That's the man."

Moriarty was one of three brothers. One was a station master in the West Country; the other—also named James by an unimaginative Mrs. Moriarty—was an army colonel by the time of the final confrontation.

The Professor pursued an academic career to begin with—and to this day there are Holmes scholars who believe that Holmes and Mycroft may have passed briefly under his tutelage.

Holmes spoke relatively little about Moriarty until just before his 'death' in "The Final Problem," at which time he told Watson . . .

"His career has been an extraordinary one. He is a man of good birth and excellent education, endowed by Nature with a phenomenal mathematical faculty. At the age of twenty-one he wrote a treatise upon the Binomial Theory, which had a European vogue. On the strength of it, he won the Mathematical Chair at one of our smaller universities, and had to all appearance, a most brilliant career before him."

Somewhere along the line he also found time to write a book, *The Dynamics of the Asteroid*—a treatise which, in Holmes's view, ascended "to such rarified heights of pure mathematics that it is said that there was no man in the scientific press capable of critiquing it."

"But the man had hereditary tendencies of the most diabolical kind. A criminal strain ran in his blood, which, instead of being modified, was increased and rendered infinitely more dangerous by his extraordinary mental powers. Dark rumours gathered round him in the University town and eventually he was compelled to resign his Chair and to come down to London."

It was there that his path crossed with Holmes . . .

"For years past I have continually been conscious of some power behind the malefactor, some deep organising power which for ever stands in the way of the law, and throws its shield over the wrong-doer. Again and again in cases of the most varying sorts—forgery cases, robberies, murders—I have felt the presence of this force, and I have deduced its actions in many of those undiscovered crimes in which I have not been personally consulted. For years I have endeavoured to break through the veil which shrouded it, and at last the time came when I seized my thread and followed it, until it led me, after a thousand cunning windings, to ex-Professor of mathematical celebrity."

Holmes also likened Moriarty's network to "a chain with this Napoleon-gone-wrong at one end and a hundred broken fighting men, pickpockets, blackmailers and card-sharpers at the other, with every sort of crime in between . . ." He was a man who had "all the powers of darkness at his back."

[In *The Valley of Fear*, [1888] where Holmes first mentions Moriarty, he compares the Professor to the famous eighteenth-century villain, Jonathan Wild, who also came to control much of London's criminal *milieu* . . . "the hidden force of the London criminals, to whom he sold his brains and his organisation on a fifteen per cent commission. The old wheel turns and the same spoke comes up. It's all been done before and will be again." But Wild, unlike Moriarty, was eventually caught, tried and executed.]

As early as 1888 Holmes is pursuing Moriarty to his lair. In *The Valley of Fear* he tells Watson and Inspector MacDonald . . .

"I have been three times in his rooms, twice waiting for him under different names and leaving before he came. How did he acquire wealth? He is unmarried. His young brother is a station master in the West of England. His Chair is worth seven hundred a year . . . dozens of exiguous threads which lead vaguely towards the centre of the web where the poisonous creature is lurking! don't say he can't be beat. But you must give me time—you must give me time!(He is) the greatest schemer of all time, the organiser of every devilry, the controlling brain of the underworld—a brain that might have made or marred the destiny of nations . . . If I am spared by lesser men our day will surely come."

In Moriarty it is possible that Holmes saw his own *alter ego*. In a perverse way he admired the man. "My horror at his crimes," he would tell Watson, "was lost in my admiration for his skill."

"When you have one of the finest brains in Europe up against you . . . there are infinite possibilities." (*The Valley of Fear*)

To which MacDonald—who had actually met the Professor—replied, expressing what was presumably a generally held feeling—"We think in the CID that you have a wee bit of a bee in your bonnet over this Professor . . . He'd have made a grand meenister, with his thin face and grey hair and solemn-like way of talking. When he put his hand on my shoulder as we were parting, it was like a father's blessing before you go out into the cold, cruel world."

And if the beady Scot, who was nobody's fool, could be so mistaken, Holmes had proved his point. It was to take another three years before he could feel confident enough to say—"My nets are closing upon him."

By that time the dossier was complete. Holmes could not estimate Moriarty's resources in detail but the existence of twenty or more banking accounts had been uncovered with "the bulk of his fortune abroad in the Deutsche Bank or the Crédit Lyonnais, as likely as not." He was also known to own a painting by Greuze whose work by now realized in the region of £40,000 at auction.

In 1891 matters came to a head. Realizing that Holmes was closing in on him, Moriarty paid him a visit at 221b . . .

"My nerves are fairly proof, Watson, but I must confess to a start when I saw the very man who had been so much in my thoughts standing there on my threshold. His appearance was quite familiar to me. He is extremely tall and thin, his forehead domes out in a white curve and his two eyes are deeply sunken in his head. He is clean-shaven, pale, and ascetic-looking, retaining something of the professor in his features. His shoulders are rounded from much study, and his face protrudes forward and is forever slowly oscillating from side to side in a curiously reptilian fashion."

Moriarty addresses him—"You hope to beat me. I tell you that you will never beat me. If you are clever enough to bring destruction upon me, rest assured that I shall do as much to you."

To which Holmes replied—"You have paid me several compliments, Mr. Moriarty . . . (note the deliberate omission of his title) . . . Let me pay you one in return when I say that if I were assured of the former eventuality I would, in the interest of the public, cheerfully accept the latter."

*   *   *   *

On April 24 of that year the opportunity came. Holmes handed the threads of his net to the official authorities and paid a visit to his old friend, by now married and in private practice. He repeated the sentiments he had expressed to Moriarty:

"I tell you, Watson, in all seriousness, that if I could beat that man, if I could free society of him, I should feel that my own career had reached its summit, and I should be prepared to turn to some more placid line in life . . . I could continue to live in the quiet fashion which is most congenial to me, and to concentrate my attention upon my chemical researches. But I could not rest, Watson, I could not sit quiet in my chair, if I thought that such a man as Professor Moriarty were walking the streets of London unchallenged." He then proceeded to brief Watson fully for the first time.

All the plans were in place for the capture of "ex-Professor Moriarty of mathematical celebrity" and his gang, but "a few days remain before the police are at liberty to act." Holmes, having decided that a discretionary absence is the better part of senseless valor, proposes that Watson accompany him to the Continent for a week while the net closes. They arrange to meet next morning at Victoria Station "in time for the continental express."

Next morning, as arranged, "a brougham was waiting with a very massive driver wrapped in a dark cloak." Only later, when Holmes enlightened him, did Watson discover that the "massive" driver was, in fact, Mycroft.

Despite their precautions, Moriarty's men—who had set fire to the Baker Street rooms the previous evening—almost overtake them at the station as the train is pulling away. Holmes then makes a drastic change of plan. Knowing that Moriarty will charter a 'special' to follow and catch up with them at the coast, he and Watson leave the express at Canterbury. There, from behind a pile of luggage, they watch the special flash past. It was Watson's first sighting of the Napoleon of Crime.

By anticipating the Professor they have gained a temporary respite. ("It would have been a *coup-de-mâitre* had he deduced what I would deduce and acted accordingly.")

For the next week the two friends crisscross Europe, finishing up in Switzerland, "by way of Interlaken, to Meiringen," where they arrived on May 3, putting up at the Englischer Hof. By this time they have learned that the police have rounded up all of the rank and file of Moriarty's gang—except the Professor himself. A variety of 'incidents' tell Holmes that the pursuit continues. "We could not walk ourselves clear of the danger which was dogging our footsteps."

Strangely—it seems to Watson—Holmes seems less and less concerned. "I can never recollect having seen him in such exuberant spirits." But he is also in reflective mood:

"I think I may go so far as to say, Watson, that I have not lived wholly in vain. If my record were closed tonight I could still survey it with equanimity. The air of London is the sweeter for my presence. In over a thousand cases I am not aware that I have ever used my powers upon the wrong side. Of late, I have been tempted to look into the problems furnished by Nature rather than those more superficial ones for which our artificial state of society is responsible. Your memoirs will draw to an end, Watson, upon the day that I crown my career by the capture or extinction of the most dangerous and capable criminal in Europe."

That day turned out to be May 4. Holmes and Watson go out for a walk to the Hamlet of Rosenlaui, taking a detour to see the famous falls of Reichenbach . . .

"It is, indeed, a fearful place. The torrent, swollen by the melting snow, plunges into a tremendous abyss, from which the spray rolls up like the smoke from a burning building."

As they reach their destination, a messenger from the hotel arrives with a request for Watson to return to help with a medical emergency. "As I turned away I saw Holmes with his back against a rock and his arms folded, gazing down at the rush of waters. It was the last that I was ever destined to see of him in this world."

On his way down Watson has his second and last encounter with Moriarty. Along a curving path "a man was, I remember, walking very rapidly. I could see his black figure clearly outlined against the green behind him. I noted him, and the energy with which he walked, but he passed from my mind again as I hurried on upon my errand."

The "errand," of course, turned out to be a false one and simply a means to distract Watson and leave Holmes alone to face his nemesis.

The world knows what supposedly happened next. Returning to the scene, Watson found that "two lines of footmarks were clearly marked along the further end of the path, both leading away from me. There were none returning." There was one other thing— a scribbled note from Holmes lying under "the silver cigarette-case which he used to carry . . ."

"MY DEAR WATSON,

I write these few lines through the courtesy of Mr. Moriarty, who awaits my convenience for the final discussion of those questions which lie between us. He has been giving me a sketch of the methods by which he avoided the English police and kept himself informed of our movements. They certainly confirm the very high opinion which I had formed of his abilities. I am pleased to think that I shall be able to free society from any further effects of his presence, though I fear that it is at a cost which will give pain to my friends, and especially, my dear Watson, to you. I have already explained to you, however, that my career had in any case reached its crisis, and that no possible conclusion to it could be more congenial to me than this. Indeed, if I may make a full confession to you, I was quite convinced that the letter from Meiringen was a hoax, and I allowed you to depart on that errand under the persuasion that some development of this sort would follow. Tell Inspector Patterson that the papers which he needs to convict the gang are in pigeon-hole M., done up in a blue envelope and inscribed 'Moriarty.' I made every disposition of my property before leaving England, and handed it to my brother, Mycroft. Pray give my greetings to Mrs. Watson, and believe me to be, my dear fellow,

Very sincerely yours,
SHERLOCK HOLMES"

"And there, deep down in that dreadful cauldron of swirling water and seething foam, will lie for all time the most dangerous criminal and the foremost champion of the law of their generation . . . him whom I shall ever regard as the best and the wisest man whom I have ever known." ("The Final Problem")

(In using these words Watson—unconsciously or not—was echoing Plato's words on the death of Socrates . . . "Such was the end . . . of our friend, who was . . . of all those of his time whom we have ever known, the best and wisest and most righteous man.")

There were three accounts of Holmes's death, including the *Journal de Genève* (May 6, 1899) and the Reuter's dispatch carried by English papers on May 7.

*   *   *   *

But neither Holmes nor Watson was to be done with Moriarty.

In 1893 Watson was forced to write "The Final Problem." "It was my intention . . . to have said nothing of that event which has created a void in my life which the lapse of two years has done little to fill. My hand has been forced, however, by the recent letters in which Colonel James Moriarty defends the memory of his brother, and I have no choice but to lay the facts before the public exactly as they occurred."

A year later Holmes made his dramatic return and—"for the first and last time in my life"—Watson fainted. In the adventure of

The death of Sherlock Holmes at the Reichenbach Falls. (Sidney Paget for "The Final Problem," 1893)

"The Empty House"—as we have seen—Colonel Moran and the last of Moriarty's stragglers were rounded up—after which Holmes claimed to suffer to some degree from a sense of anti-climax for the remainder of his career . . .

"From the point of view of the criminal expert, London has become a singularly uninteresting city since the death of the late lamented Professor Moriarty." ("The Norwood Builder, " 1895)

But was it really as simple as all that?

After all, if Holmes was able to escape and go to ground for three whole years, is it impossible that a man as ingenious as Moriarty could not have contrived a similar feat?

And while Holmes needed the limelight of London and the criminal world required the *imprimatur* of his presence, Moriarty's preferred *modus operandi* was anonymity. Had he survived, it is hardly likely that he would have advertised the fact. Perhaps that devious mind saw supreme advantage in not repossessing his original persona.

And when one considers the terrible and tangled web of events that have happened to the world *since* that day at Reichenbach . . .

"What is the meaning of it, Watson? What object is served by this circle of misery and violence and fear? It must tend to some end, or else our universe is ruled by chance, which is unthinkable. But what end? There is the great . . . perennial problem to which human reason is as far from an answer as ever." ("The Cardboard Box")

Or is it?

The "Insoluble Puzzle"

"Woman's heart and mind are insoluble puzzles to the male. Murder might be condoned or explained and yet some small offences might rankle."

—"The Illustrious Client"

"The motives of women are so inscrutable ... How can you build on such a quicksand? Their most trivial action may mean volumes, or their most extraordinary conduct may depend upon a hairpin or a curling-tongs."

—"The Second Stain"

HOLMES WOULD HAVE found it hard to cope with our politically correct times, for basically he did not trust them as a sex. "I am not a whole-souled admirer of womankind, as you are aware, Watson ..." (*The Valley of Fear*) "Women are never to be entirely trusted—not the best of them." (*The Sign of Four*) They were anathema because they believed in the pre-eminence of emotion . . . and in particular that age-old devastating disease called—love . . .

"Love is an emotional thing, and whatever is emotional is opposed to that true, cold reason which I place above all things. I should never marry myself, lest I bias my judgement." (*The Sign of Four*) . . . "I have never loved, Watson . . ." ("The Devil's Foot") . . . "Women have seldom been an attraction to me, for my brain has always governed my heart . . ." ("The Lion's Mane") . . . "The emotional qualities are antagonistic to clear reasoning." (*The Sign of Four*) "The lady's charming personality must not be permitted to warp our judgment." ("The Abbey Grange")

"He disliked and distrusted the sex, but he was always a chivalrous opponent." In fact, he protests so much it has led some commentators to the view that Holmes may have been disappointed in love at an early age and determined to have none of it.

But despite his reservations . . .

"Holmes had, when he liked, a peculiarly ingratiating way with women and he very readily established terms of confidence with them." ("The Golden Pince-Nez")

And just because he was distrustful of them, his logical mind did not dismiss what they had to offer to his work . . . "I value a woman's instinct in these matters" ("The Lion's Mane") . . . "No woman would have sent a reply-paid telegram. She would have come." ("Wisteria Lodge") . . . "Women are naturally secretive, and they like to do their own secreting." ("A Scandal in Bohemia") . . . "I have seen too much not to know that the impression of a woman may be more valuable than the conclusions of an analytical reasoner." ("The Man with the Twisted Lip")

But however much he had seen, it was not enough to solve all the mysteries of the Sphinx. In "The Second Stain" Holmes deduced that a woman whom he observed to have "manoeuvred to have the light at her back" had done so in order to conceal the expression on her face. In fact, all that she was trying to conceal was the fact that she had "no powder on her nose." When this became clear, he considered it ample proof of the inscrutability of women's motives.

It would occasionally amuse him to cast Watson in the role of the ladies' man . . . "'Now, Watson, the fair sex is your department,' said Holmes with a smile, when the dwindling *frou-frou* of skirts had ended" ("The Second Stain") "With your natural advantages, Watson, every lady is your helper and accomplice." ("Shoscombe Old Place") . . . and to tease him on the subject. When Watson first meets Mary Morstan—soon to be (the second ?) Mrs. Watson—in *The Sign of Four* and exclaims "What a very attractive woman!"— Holmes "had lit his pipe again and was leaning back with drooping eyelids. 'Is she?'" he said languidly. 'I did not observe.'"

"You really are an automaton—a calculating machine. There is something positively inhuman about you at times," is Watson's appropriate reply. Holmes, however, has a logical rationale for his attitude . . . "It is the first importance not to allow your judgement to be biased by personal qualities. A client to me is a mere unit, a factor in a problem. The emotional qualities are antagonistic to clear reasoning. I assure you that the most winning woman I ever knew was hanged for poisoning three little children for their insurance money."

Nonetheless, there are occasional hints that Holmes did allow himself to contemplate the possibility, however briefly . . .

"I thought of her (Violet de Merville) for a moment as I would have thought of a daughter of my own. I am not often eloquent. I use my head, not my heart. But I really did plead with her with all the warmth of words that I could find in my nature." ("The Illustrious Client")

"You owe a very humble apology to that noble lad, your son, who has carried himself in this matter as I should be proud to see my own son do, should I ever chance to have one." ("The Beryl Coronet")

In "Charles Augustus Milverton" Holmes is forced to adopt extreme measures to defeat the 'King of Blackmailers.' He temporarily adopts the persona of Escott, a young plumber with prospects, and wins the heart of Milverton's maid, Agatha, so as to obtain information about her employer. Since his efforts result in his becoming engaged to the girl, one might well speculate to what lengths Holmes had to go to fulfill his mission. Watson, however, is appropriately discreet on the subject—but the constraints of Victorian middle class morality were such that—verbal commitment probably sufficed.

"'You would not call me a marrying man, Watson?'

'No, indeed!'

'You'll be interested to know that I'm engaged.'

'My dear fellow! I congrat—'

'To Milverton's housemaid.'

'Good heavens, Holmes!'

'I have walked out with her each evening, and I have talked with her. Good heavens, those talks! However, I have got all I wanted.'

'But the girl, Holmes?'

He shrugged his shoulders.

'You can't help it, my dear Watson. You must play your cards as best you can . . .'"

There was one woman whom Holmes admired for her dignity in distress—Eugenia Ronder, the "Veiled Lodger"—"(He) stretched out his long arm and patted her hand with such a show of sympathy as I had seldom known him to exhibit." . . . and one for her beauty—Maud Bellamy ("The Lion's Mane") who was "the beauty of the (Sussex) neighbourhood" during his retirement, so much so "that no young man would cross her path unscathed." [Perhaps if the mellower and more observant Holmes had been younger . . .]

. . . and one for whom Watson would clearly have liked him to show more interest—Miss Violet Hunter, heroine of "The Copper Beeches," with her "bright, quick face" and the "brisk manner of a woman who has had her way to make in the world." "My friend Holmes, rather to my disappointment, manifested no further interest in her when once she had ceased to be the centre of one of his problems." Even though Holmes had initially observed that she was "a woman with a mind."

Watson's 'disappointment' may have been influenced by the fact that Miss Hunter is the only one of Holmes's female clients who distinctly flirts with him.

When she first meets him, she finds a way to tell him of her qualifications . . . "A little French, a little German, music and drawing . . ." and then draws his attention to her appearance . . . "As you may observe, Mr. Holmes, my hair is somewhat luxuriant, and of a rather peculiar tint of chestnut. It has been considered artistic." Then later—"I am naturally observant, as you may have observed, Mr. Holmes." Of course, it may simply be that since Watson is relating what happened, he is exercising his own selective memory of the lady's charms, which, had he not been a respectable married man himself at the time, he might have pursued further. Miss Hunter, he informs us, went on to be "the head of a private school at Walsall, where I believe she has met with considerable success."

*   *   *   *

But for Holmes there was only ever *one* woman—*the* woman. Irene Adler from "A Scandal in Bohemia." The only woman who ever beat him. Forever sandwiched in his commonplace book between Chief Rabbi Adler and an anonymous sailor, the American born opera singer and adventuress consistently managed

"Holmes shook his head gravely." Miss Violet Hunter "had the brisk manner of a woman who has had her way to make in the world." (Sidney Paget for "The Copper Beeches," 1892)

to wrongfoot him by anticipating and playing him at his own game—even to the point of deceiving him in male disguise. When the King of Bohemia wished to reward him—for what was at most a very qualified success—Holmes accepted a jeweled snuff box but what he valued infinitely more was the photograph of Irene Adler.

At first glance even Holmes was suitably impressed, for he reported to Watson that she was "the daintiest thing under a bonnet on this planet."

"To Sherlock Holmes she is always *the* woman."—Watson records—"I have seldom heard him mention her under any other name. In his eyes she eclipses and predominates the whole of her sex. It was not that he felt any emotion akin to love . . . All emotions, and that one particularly, were abhorrent to his cold, precise, but admirable balanced mind. He was, I take it, the most perfect reasoning and observing machine that the world has seen. He never spoke of the softer passions, save with a jibe and a sneer . . . for the trained observer to admit such intrusions into his own delicate and finely adjusted temperament was to introduce a distracting factor which might throw a doubt upon all his mental results. Grit in a sensitive instrument, or a crack in one of his own high-power lenses, would not be more disturbing than a strong emotion in a nature such as his."

When the case was over, though, Watson would add . . .

"He used to make merry over the cleverness of women, but I have not heard him do it of late. And when he refers to her photograph, it is always under the honourable title of *the* woman."

And while feminists are never likely to regard Holmes as anything approaching a positive icon. . . . "She has flown to tea as an agitated woman will" ("The Crooked Man") . . . they may regard Irene Adler's achievement as one small step for womankind.

"Goodnight, Mr. Sherlock Holmes."

"I've heard that voice before," said Holmes.

Irene Adler defeats the master of disguise at his own game. (Sidney Paget for "A Scandal in Bohemia," 1891)

Irene Adler—"*the* woman." (Unknown French artists, c. 1920)

"My Dear Watson"

"It may be that you are not yourself luminous, but you are a conductor of light. Some people without possessing genius have a remarkable power of stimulating it."

—*The Hound of the Baskervilles*

"Come, Watson, come! The game is afoot."

IT'S TEMPTING TO think that the relationship between Holmes and Watson was set once and for all on the day they moved into 221b Baker Street but the evidence is otherwise.

In fact, they experienced the same sea changes that affect any close relationship. Sometimes they bored one another; occasionally they infuriated one another; but always each was deeply concerned for the wellbeing of the other.

Not surprisingly, over time the more mercurial one (Holmes) tended to take the more predictable one (Watson) for granted. Not long before Holmes's retirement Watson summed up the state of their friendship in particularly perceptive fashion:

"There's our man, Watson! Come along." (Sidney Paget for *The Hound of the Baskervilles*, 1902)

"The relations between us in those latter days were peculiar. He was a man of habits, narrow and concentrated habits, and I had become one of them. As an institution I was like the violin, the shag tobacco, the old black pipe, the index books, and others perhaps less excusable. When it was a case of active work and a comrade was needed upon whose nerve he could place some reliance, my role was obvious. But apart from this I had uses. I was a whetstone for his mind. I stimulated him. He liked to think aloud in my presence. His remarks could hardly be said to be made to me—many of them would have been as appropriately addressed to his bedstead—but none the less, having formed the habit, it has become in some way helpful that I should register and interject. If I irritated him by a certain methodical slowness in my mentality, that irritation only served to make his own flame-like intuitions and impressions flash up the more vividly and swiftly. Such was my humble role in our alliance."

That alliance lasted for twenty-three of the years Holmes was in active practice and he and Watson shared the Baker Street 'digs' for seventeen of those. The accumulated evidence of those years would suggest that in those years Watson's role was anything but "humble." Holmes needed Watson more than Watson needed Holmes. In fact, it could well be argued that if there had been no Watson, there would have been no Holmes as we know him. His own insecurities would have devoured him.

*   *   *   *

John H. Watson was born probably in 1852, somewhere in the south of England, despite his Scottish ancestry. Certainly, when he returns from his military service, he gravitates towards London and the home counties. (What the 'H' stood for is open to debate. One view is that it was the Scots 'Hamish,' since Mary Morstan

Watson once called him by the affectionate English diminutive 'James.' 'Henry' was a popular name at the time but then, Watson's father and older brother shared that name and even though the Moriarty brothers practiced such an economy . . . There were at least three boys, since Holmes refers to 'Henry' as Watson's "eldest brother.")

Watson's mother passed away when he was still young and the family emigrated to Australia, where he gained his knowledge of the goldfields that he demonstrates in *The Sign of Four*. He must have returned to England around 1865.

We know nothing of his general education, except that he was at school with Percy 'Tadpole' Phelps (who appears in "The Naval Treaty"). Since Phelps's uncle was Lord Holdhurst, "the great Conservative politician," it's safe to assume one of the better public schools was involved and, while there, he must have done sufficiently well to qualify to study medicine at London University.

After school and before university he may well have decided to travel and see something of the world—otherwise there would have been no opportunity for him to have gained the experience of women of "many nations and three separate continents" that he untypically boasts about in *The Sign of Four*.

He was the extrovert to Holmes's introvert and as a young man an enthusiastic rugby player, turning out for Blackheath among other teams. He was—he tells us—"reckoned fleet of foot." In "The Sussex Vampire" he meets one of his old opponents, Big Bob Ferguson, "the finest three-quarter Richmond ever had," who, in his heyday, had known the strapping young Watson. By the time of their reunion in 1896 Watson is even more strapping and Ferguson remarks—"You don't look quite the man you did when I threw you over the ropes into the crowd at the old Deer Park." In later years, however, he and his old friends had tended to drift apart.

"In the year 1878 I took my degree of Doctor of Medicine at the University of London, and proceeded to Netley to go through the course prescribed for surgeons in the army. Having completed my studies there, I was duly attached to the Fifth Northumberland Fusiliers as Assistant Surgeon. The regiment was stationed in India at the time, and before I could join it, the second Afghan War had broken out. On landing at Bombay, I learned that my corps had advanced through the passes, and was already deep in the enemy's country. I followed, however, with many other officers who were in the same situation as myself, and succeeded in reaching Candahar in safety, where I found my regiment, and at once entered into my new duties."

"The campaign brought honours and promotion to many, but for me it had nothing but misfortune and disaster. I was removed from my brigade and attached to the Berkshires, with whom I served at the fatal battle of Maiwand (July 27, 1880). There I was struck on the shoulder by a Jezail bullet, which shattered the bone and grazed the subclavian artery . . ."

[In later years Watson's memory was again inclined to play him tricks. In *The Sign of Four* he is "nursing my wounded leg. I had had a Jezail bullet through it some time before." But in "The Noble Bachelor" he was less specific and he would only recall the bullet "which I had brought back in one of my limbs as a result of my Afghan campaign." From which one can only conclude that perhaps he had taken two bullets during that dire time and simply forgotten to mention one of them earlier. Or perhaps only one of them 'played him up.']

"I should have fallen into the hands of the murderous Ghazis had it not been for the devotion and courage shown by Murray, my orderly, who threw me across a packhorse, and succeeded in bringing me safely to the British lines."

"Worn with pain, and weak from the prolonged hardships which I had undergone, I was removed, with a great train of wounded sufferers, to the base hospital at Peshawur. Here I rallied, and had already improved so far as to be able to walk about the wards, and even to bask a little upon a verandah, when I was struck down with enteric fever, that curse of our Indian possessions. For months my life was despaired of, and when at last I came to myself and became convalescent, I was so weak and emaciated that a medical board determined that not a day should be lost in sending me back to England. I was despatched, accordingly, on the troopship *Orontes*, and landed a month later on Portsmouth jetty, with my health irretrievably ruined, but with permission from a paternal government to spend the next nine months attempting to improve it."

Thus ended Watson's War.

* * * *

We have no detailed physical description of Watson—not surprisingly, since he is the one who narrates most of the stories. When he meets young Stamford in the Criterion Bar, Stamford exclaims that Watson is "as thin as a lath and as brown as a nut"—but, once he is safely ensconced in 221b with Mrs. Hudson's good plain cooking, the impression one derives (and one borne out by most of the contemporary illustrations) is of a stockily-built man of rather more than middle height. At the time of the Milverton affair (1899?) Lestrade describes him as "a middle-sized, strongly-built man—square jaw, thick neck, moustache . . . " In later years, unlike Holmes, he tended to put on weight—a tendency not helped by marriage and a social life that largely centered around his chair in Baker Street and a decent bottle of Beaune and a game of billiards with his friend, Thurston, at his club. When he and Holmes have to chase

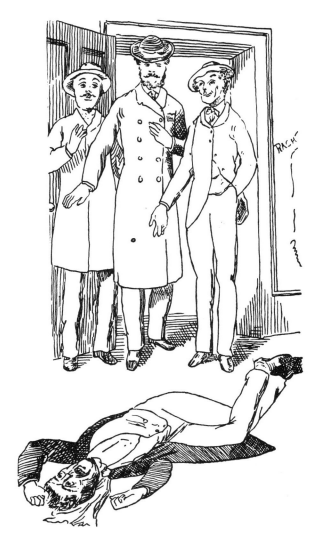

"The single, grim, motionless figure . . . lay stretched upon the boards."
Watson, a bearded Holmes, and Inspector Lestrade investigate. (One of the
six drawings done by Charles Altamont Doyle, father of Conan Doyle, for
A *Study in Scarlet*, 1888)

after a dog-cart in "The Solitary Cyclist" (1895) . . . "my sedentary life began to tell on me and I was compelled to fall behind."

Nor did the old war wounds help, although they never deterred him from pocketing his old service revolver—the Adams .450 Standard Army Issue—and following wherever his old friend led.

He was pleasant looking rather than conventionally handsome and particularly proud of his moustache. Holmes referred to it as "modest" but that was clearly a clean-shaven man's lack of appreciation for well-tended and somewhat luxurious facial hair.

A pipe smoker like Holmes, Watson continued to favor "the Arcadia mixture of (his) bachelor days." His tobacco was supplied by Bradley's and the firm also provided his cigarettes: "When I see the stub of a cigarette marked Bradley, Oxford Street, I know that my friend Watson is in the neighbourhood." A creature of habit in other ways, too, he learned to put up with Holmes's teasing on the subject—"It's easy to tell that you've been accustomed to wearing a uniform, Watson; you'll never pass as a pure-bred civilian as long as you keep that habit of carrying your handkerchief in your sleeve." ("The Crooked Man")

The military habits die hard in an old soldier and Watson was always neatly dressed. When out and about he invariably wore an ulster and was never seen without a hat.

Around 221b he affected patent leather slippers—a rare touch of vanity. Like Holmes, however, "I had a weakness for the Turkish bath." ("The Illustrious Client")

By no stretch of the imagination was he an intellectual. Apart from *The British Medical Journal*, his daily reading was the *Daily Telegraph*, *The Standard*, *The Daily News*, and—more intensively—the racing paper. When it came to more formal literature, he had a weakness for sea stories. On one occasion ("Boscombe Valley")—perhaps to pick up a few pointers from one writer to

"Holmes pulled out his watch." (Sidney Paget for "The Naval Treaty," 1893)

"I tried to interest myself in a yellow-backed novel." (Sidney Paget for "The Boscombe Valley Mystery," 1891)

another—he tried a "yellow-backed novel" but found it too thin and trashy for his taste and soon threw it aside.

One of his few 'vices' appears to have been gambling . . .

"'By the way, Watson, you know something of racing?'

'I ought to. I pay for it with about half my wound pension.'" ("Shoscombe Old Place")

In 1898—at the time of "The Dancing Men"—there is a reference to Watson's checkbook being locked up in Holmes's desk with the detective keeping the key.

*   *   *   *

During his sojourn at 221B Watson lived a double life for much of the time. He very much had an eye for the ladies. Discounting his "three continents" claim as being, at the very least, an exaggeration and setting aside Holmes's teasing "the fair sex is *your* department," it is entirely credible that . . .

"With your natural advantages, Watson, every lady is your helper and accomplice. What about the girl at the post office, or the wife of the greengrocer? I can picture you whispering soft nothings with the young lady at the 'Blue Anchor,' and receiving hard somethings in exchange." A description that from someone else would sound positively coarse.

Global *roué* or no, there is something charming and naïve about Watson's reaction to meeting Mary Morstan in *The Sign of Four*.

"She was a blonde young lady, small, dainty, well gloved, and dressed in the most perfect taste. There was, however, a plainness and simplicity about her costume which bore with it a suggestion of limited means . . . Her face had neither regularity of feature nor beauty of complexion, but her expression was sweet and amiable, and her large blue eyes were singularly spiritual and sympathetic. In an experience of women . . . etc., etc . . . I have never looked upon a face which gave a clearer promise of a refined and sensitive nature."

The impression Miss Morstan made was clearly discombobulating to the Watson psyche . . . "To this day she declares that I told her one moving anecdote as to how a musket looked into my tent at dead of night, and how I fired a double-barrelled tiger cub at it." It was literally love at first sight and a simple, uncomplicated love at that . . . "So we stood hand-in-hand, like two children."

Holmes was not best pleased when Watson announced his intention to marry the lady, though he came to accept her in time.

"'Miss Morstan has done me the honour to accept me as a husband in prospective.'" He gave a most dismal groan. 'I feared as much,' said he."

At the time of "A Scandal in Bohemia" Watson would report—"My marriage had drifted us away from each other. My own complete happiness, and the home-centred interests which rise up around the man who first finds himself master of his own establishment, were sufficient to absorb all my attention."

When Holmes sees his uxorious old friend, though, he is compelled to deduce that "'Wedlock suits you . . . I think, Watson, that you have put on seven and a half pounds since I saw you.'

'Seven.' I answered."

Watson and Mary were married in May 1889 and there are those who would have it that she was his *second* wife. Their theory is that he married an American, one Constance Adams, in late 1886 and moved out of Baker Street. (He may have met her when he was in practice in San Francisco.) When the first Mrs. Watson died a year later, he returned to his old quarters. This view, it should be said, is strongly disputed by many scholars.

At the time of their marriage Watson again left Baker Street and took on a practice near Paddington Station, purchased from

"Old Farquhar." Although he would say that "My practice is never very absorbing," he nevertheless managed to build it up nicely until he had a "fairly long list" of patients. In consequence, he saw less and less of Holmes, "although I continually visited him, and occasionally even persuaded him to forego his Bohemian habits so far as to come and visit us." In 1890 he would record only three of Holmes's cases in which he had been personally involved. ("The Naval Treaty," "The Second Stain," and "The Retired Colourman.") Though when the great call did come and the game was once more afoot, he could always count on Dr. Anstruther or Dr. Jackson to fill in as *locum*.

The Watsons enjoyed a happy marriage, though sadly, a brief one. Mary Morstan Watson died somewhere during Holmes's absence. Of what cause Watson finds it too painful to relate but she can only have been in her early thirties at most. The most likely cause would appear to be either that prevalent illness the Victorians called 'consumption' (tuberculosis), which might account for her frequent absences "on a visit to her aunt" or "away on a visit" or a heart condition she may have inherited from her father. Those visits may well have been to a sanitarium for treatment. On Holmes's return it is clear that he has learned of his friend's "sad bereavement and his sympathy was shown in his manner rather than in his words.'Work is the best antidote to sorrow, my dear Watson,' said he . . ."

Watson had been trying to do just that in his practice—as well as keeping his hand in by attempting to solve the occasional reported crime by Holmesian methods. ("It can be imagined that my close intimacy with Sherlock Holmes had interested me deeply in crime, and that after his disappearance I never failed to read with care the various problems which came before the public, and I even attempted more than once for my own private satisfaction to employ his methods in their solution, though with indifferent success.")

It does not take long for Holmes to persuade his old partner to sell his practice—a new one now in Kensington—and to move back into the familiar quarters. [Only later does Watson learn that the accommodating young Dr. Vernet who is prepared to pay "with astonishingly little demur the highest price that he ventured to ask for the practice" is a distant relation of the Holmes (Vernet) family, using money provided by Holmes himself.]

Then followed eight years of great activity, as case followed case. But in 1902 Watson had sufficiently recovered from his grief after ten years to marry again. In January ("The Blanched Soldier") Holmes is relating that "the good Watson . . . had deserted me for a wife, the only selfish action which I can recall in our association. I was alone."

The fact that he considered this one "selfish," and not the marriage to Mary Morstan, is telling. So is the fact that Watson himself never tells us anything about the new "Mrs. Watson." How long they were married, whether she outlived him (unlikely, considering the mortality rate of his previous spouses) . . . all remains in the realm of the unknown. What we do know is that she did not stand in the way of her husband's friendship with Holmes, for the two men were solving puzzles well into 1903 and Holmes's retirement.

* * * *

Watson had early personal experience of his friend's remarkable deductive powers.

Early in *The Sign of Four* he determines to test Holmes's powers:

"'Now, I have here a watch which has recently come into my possession. Would you have the kindness to let me have an opinion upon the character or habits of the late owner?'

'Subject to your correction, I should judge that the watch belonged to your elder brother, who inherited it from your father.'

'That you gather, no doubt, from the HW upon the back?'

'Quite so. The W suggests your own name. The date of the watch is nearly fifty years back and the initials are as old as the watch; so it was made for the last generation. Jewellery usually descends to the eldest son, and he is most likely to have the same name as the father. Your father has, if I remember right, been dead many years. It has, therefore, been in the hands of your eldest brother.'

'Right so far,' said I. 'Anything else?'

'He was a man of untidy habits—very untidy and careless. He was left with good prospects, but he threw away his chances, lived for some time in poverty with occasional short intervals of prosperity, and, finally, turning to drink, he died. That is all I can gather.'

Watson is duly amazed . . .

'Then how in the name of all that is wonderful did you get these facts? They are absolutely correct in every particular.'

Holmes explains . . .

"For example, I began by stating that your brother was careless. When you observe the lower part of that watch-case you notice that it is not only dented in two places, but it is cut and marked all over from the habit of keeping other hard objects, such as coins or keys, in the same pocket. Surely it is no great feat to assume that a man who treats a fifty-guinea watch so cavalierly must be a careless man. Neither is it a very far-fetched inference that a man who inherits one article of such value is pretty well provided for in other respects.'

I nodded, to show that I followed his reasoning.

'It is very customary for pawnbrokers in England, when they take a watch, to scratch the number of the ticket with a pin-point upon the inside of the case. It is more handy than a label, as there is no risk of the number being lost or transposed. There are no less than four such numbers visible to my lens on the inside of this case. Inference—that your brother was often at low water. Secondary inference—that he had occasional bursts of prosperity, or he could not have redeemed the pledge. Finally, I ask you to look at the inner plate which contains the keyhole. Look at the thousands of scratches all round the hole—marks where the key has slipped. What sober man's keys could have scored those grooves? But you will never see a drunkard's watch without them. He winds it at night, and he leaves these traces of his unsteady hand. Where is the mystery in all this?'"

From then on he was a willing pupil to Holmes the master but the relationship was not as one-sided as it might appear.

Holmes needed a sparring partner to sharpen his own skills . . .

"This is my friend and colleague, Dr. Watson who is occasionally good enough to help me in my cases . . . you may say before this gentleman anything which you may say to me." ("A Scandal in Bohemia")

"I very much prefer having a witness, if only as a check to my own memory." ("The Noble Bachelor")

"It is really very good of you to come, Watson. It makes a considerable difference to me, having someone on whom I can thoroughly rely." ("The Boscombe Valley Mystery")

"There is no man better worth having at your side when you are in a tight place." (To Sir Henry Baskerville in The Hound of the Baskervilles)

"You are a British jury and I never met a man more eminently fitted to represent one." ("The Abbey Grange")

"At least I have got a grip of the essential facts of the case. I shall enumerate them for you, for nothing clears up a case so much as stating it to another person, and I can hardly expect your cooperation if I do not show you the position from which we start." ("Silver Blaze")

"If I burden myself with a companion in my various little enquiries, it is not done out of sentiment or caprice, but it is that Watson has some

"Holmes gave me a sketch of the events." (Sidney Paget for "Silver Blaze,"
1892)

remarkable characteristics of his own, to which in his modesty he has given small attention amid his exaggerated estimates of my own performances. A confederate who foresees your conclusions and course of action is always dangerous, but one to whom each development comes as a perpetual surprise, and to whom the future is always a closed book, is, indeed, an ideal helpmate." ("The Blanched Soldier")

Holmes, though, could rarely resist playing the magisterial role . . .

"'And what do you think of it all, Watson?' asked Sherlock Holmes, leaning back in his chair.

"I saw that he cocked his eye at me to see if I had followed his reasoning." ("The Yellow Face")

"It is true that though in your mission you have missed everything of importance, yet even those things which have obtruded themselves upon your notice give rise to serious thought." ("The Five Orange Pips")

"'Most of your conclusions were erroneous. When I said that you stimulated me I meant, to be frank, that in noting your fallacies I was occasionally guided towards the truth.'" (*The Hound of the Baskervilles*)

Very often Watson found himself depressed by Holmes's patronizing attitude . . .

"I was always oppressed with a sense of my own stupidity in my dealing with Sherlock Holmes." ("The Red-Headed League")

"I understand now what I should never have forgotten, that I am the pupil and you are the master." ("Black Peter")

"He gave no explanations and I asked for none. By long experience I had learned the wisdom of obedience . . . 'I am here to be used, Holmes.'" ("The Illustrious Client")

"It was difficult to refuse any of Holmes's requests, for they were always so exceedingly definite, and put forward with such an air of mastery." ("The Man with the Twisted Lip"). Not that he was ever

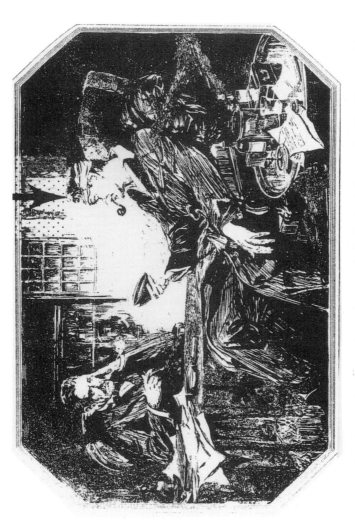

Holmes recovers from the attack of Baron Gruner's agents. (John Richard Flanagan for "The Illustrious Client," 1925)

"My dear Watson, the two events are connected—must be connected."
(Sidney Paget for "The Second Stain," 1904)

inclined to refuse, for those requests had him "tingling with that half-sporting, half-intellectual pleasure which I invariably experienced when I was associated with him in his investigations." ("The Crooked Man")

What he realized but rarely was that Holmes desperately needed him as a foil. Holmes was the pretty girl who deliberately seeks out a plain girl as her best friend, so that comparisons will be made in her favor—then finds, as in this case, that the team adds up to something infinitely greater than the sum of the parts.

Watson kept Holmes sharp . . .

"'There is an appalling directness about your questions, Watson,' said Holmes, shaking his pipe at me. 'They come at me like bullets.'" (*The Valley of Fear*)

. . . and, to be fair, Holmes invariably thought and talked in terms of 'we' and it was Holmes who sought out Watson—not the other way around . . .

"We have not yet met our Waterloo, Watson, but this is our Marengo, for it begins in defeat and ends in victory." ("The Abbey Grange")

[Marengo was the battle fought by Napoleon in 1800 against the Austrians, when he snatched victory from the jaws of defeat. Fifteen years later he lost the decisive Battle of Waterloo to the Duke of Wellington.]

"Our supreme adventure," was Holmes's description of *The Hound of the Baskervilles*.

Stamford had warned Watson at the very outset that "You do not know Sherlock Holmes yet . . . perhaps you would not care for him as a constant companion." He was unnecessarily concerned.

* * * *

"I hear of Sherlock everywhere since you became his chronicler." (Mycroft Holmes in "The Greek Interpreter")

The Shadow of Sherlock Holmes. (Sidney Paget for *The Hound of the Baskervilles*, 1902)

Watson would write that the stories he eventually published—all with Holmes's grudging consent—were chosen to "illustrate the remarkable mental qualities of my friend, Sherlock Holmes" and that he tried "to select those which presented the minimum of sensationalism."

"I know, my dear Watson, that you share my love of all that is bizarre and outside the conventions and humdrum routine of everyday life. You have shown your relish for it by the enthusiasm which has prompted you to chronicle, and, if you will excuse my saying so, somewhat to embellish so many of my own little adventures." ("The Red-Headed League)

"I will do nothing serious without my trusted comrade and biographer at my elbow." ("The Bruce-Partington Plans")

Holmes was fond of saying that he was "lost without my Boswell" but from the moment in *A Study in Scarlet* when Watson offers to write up the case, if Holmes is unwilling to do so, he was ambivalent at best about the whole process. It stroked his vanity but ruffled his sense of the scientific . . .

"Detection is, or ought to be, an exact science, and should be treated in the same cold and emotionless manner. You have attempted to tinge it with romanticism, which produces much the same effect as if you worked a love-story or an elopement into the fifth proposition of Euclid . . . some facts should be suppressed or, at least, a just sense of proportion should be observed in treating them."

To which Watson objects—"But the romance was there." (*The Sign of Four*)

Ironic, of course, that Holmes should criticize Watson for introducing romanticism, since, on another occasion, it seemed to be the very quality he sought. "Life is commonplace; the papers are sterile; audacity and romance seem to have passed forever from the criminal world." ("Wisteria Lodge")

It was to be an ongoing argument . . .

"You have erred, perhaps, in attempting to put colour and life into each of your statements, instead of confining yourself to the task of placing upon record that severe reasoning from cause to effect which is really the only notable feature about the thing . . . if I claim full justice for my art, it is because it is an impersonal thing—a thing beyond myself . . . Therefore, it is upon the logic rather than the crime that you should dwell. You have degraded what should have been a course of lectures into a series of tales . . . In avoiding the sensational, I fear that you may have bordered on the trivial . . ."

"Crime is common. Logic is rare."

"If you cast your mind back to some of those narratives with which you have afflicted a long-suffering public, you will recognise how often the grotesque had deepened into the criminal . . . there is but one step from the grotesque to the horrible." ("Wisteria Lodge")

"Your fatal habit of looking at everything from the point of view of a story instead of as a scientific exercise has ruined what might have been an instructive and even classical series of demonstrations. You slur over work of the utmost finesse and delicacy in order to dwell upon sensational details which may excite but cannot possibly instruct the reader." ("The Abbey Grange")

At which an irritated Watson finally erupts with—"Why do you not write them yourself?"

Finally, Holmes does so . . .

"'The ideas of my friend Watson, though limited, are exceedingly pertinacious. For a long time he has worried me to write an experience of my own.'

'Try it yourself, Holmes.'

'I am compelled to admit that, having taken my pen in hand, I do begin to realise that the matter must be presented in such a way as may interest the reader.'"

What Holmes finds—to his apparent surprise—is that telling a story involves its own techniques. He has to describe in detail precisely what he does. Whereas he had criticized his Boswell for "the effect of some of these little sketches of yours . . . depending as it does upon your retaining in your own hands some factors in the problem which are never imparted to the reader" ("The Creeping Man"), he now appreciates that "it was by concealing such links in the chain that Watson was enabled to produce his meretricious finales . . . Here it is that I miss my Watson. By cunning questions and ejaculations of wonder he could elevate my simple art, which is but systemised commonsense, into a prodigy." ("The Blanched Soldier")

This is a rather strange admission, since Holmes was accustomed to employing very similar *leger-de-main* when it came to presenting his feats of deduction.

After Reichenbach Watson found his friend to be even more skittish about his "little experiences." For a time Holmes forbade him from publishing any accounts at all and Watson was even driven to self-exculpation—"This resolution of mine was not due to any lack of material." . . . "I have continually been faced by difficulties caused by his own aversion to publicity."

And yet Holmes was unwilling to let them go altogether. They were, after all, a piece of posterity to fall back on after Scotland Yard had been allowed to take the official credit . . .

"Perhaps I shall get the credit also at some distant day when I permit my zealous historian to lay out his foolscap once more— eh, Watson?"

. . . and Watson's analogy to Holmes as the spoiled beauty would occasionally surface . . .

"I confess that I was irritated by the egotism which seemed to demand that every line of my pamphlet should be devoted to his own special doings. More than once during the years I had lived with him in Baker Street I had observed that a small vanity underlay my companion's quiet and didactic manner."

* * * *

Did Holmes have a sense of humor?

Undoubtedly—where other people were concerned. Part of Watson's role was to act as his 'straight man' and it pleased Holmes to tease him—usually in a fairly heavy-handed way.

There were, however, occasions when Watson turned the tables. "You have heard me speak of Professor Moriarty?" Holmes asks him in *The Valley of Fear*.

" 'The famous scientific criminal, as famous among crooks as—'

'My blushes, Watson!' Holmes murmured in a deprecating voice.

'I was about to say, as he is unknown to the public.'

'A touch! A distinct touch!' cried Holmes. 'You are developing a certain unexpected vein of pawky humour . . . against which I must learn to guard myself.' "

Later in the same narrative he refers to Watson's "native shrewdness . . . that innate cunning which is the delight of your friends . . . your Machiavellian intellect"—and one cannot help but feel he had been sufficiently stung to retaliate with a little irony of his own.

Another excellent example of the "pawky" (Scots) sense of humor occurs in "The Noble Bachelor":

WATSON: The vanishing of the lady.
HOLMES: When did she vanish, then?
WATSON: At the wedding breakfast.
HOLMES: Indeed. This is more interesting than it promised to be; quite dramatic, in fact.
WATSON: Yes; it struck me as being a little out of the common.

"I fell into a brown study." (Sidney Paget for "The Cardboard Box," 1892)

"Holmes was wont to pass frivolous comments on the blackest of crimes, for the fun of seeing if I would rise to the bait."

Holmes looked into Watson's eyes "with the peculiarly mischievous glance which was characteristic of his more imp-like moods." ("Thor Bridge")

"Your morals don't improve, Watson. You have added fibbing to your other vices." ("The Mazarin Stone")

"Excellent, Watson! Compound of the Busy Bee and Excelsior."

Sometimes the exchanges were laconic—like the telegram which read . . .

"COME AT ONCE IF CONVENIENT.
IF INCONVENIENT COME ALL THE SAME.
SHERLOCK HOLMES."

. . . sometimes sardonic . . .

"Excellent, Watson. You scintillate today . . ." ("The Illustrious Client")

WATSON: I can make neither head nor tail of the business.
HOLMES: Really! You surprise me.

. . . but whether the Great Detective could *take* a joke remains unproven.

*   *   *   *

What is beyond a doubt is that a genuine bond of affection existed between the two men. On Watson's side it was more obvious. He was a man who naturally wore his heart on his sleeve and his narratives demonstrate both the satisfactions and frustrations he experienced in their relationship.

"Sherlock Holmes was standing smiling at me across my study table."
(Sidney Paget for "The Empty House," 1903)

Holmes was more oblique. He did not trust emotion of any kind and was guarded in his expression. Even so, one can detect hints of the coded camaraderie that he felt for his "stormy petrel of crime" . . .

"Friends . . . except for yourself I have none . . . I do not encourage visitors." ("The Five Orange Pips")

"Watson and I are famous fishermen—are we not, Watson?" ("The Five Orange Pips") They were not!

"Perhaps the scent is not so cold but that two old hounds like Watson and myself may get a sniff of it." ("The Priory School")

"You have a grand gift of silence, Watson. It makes you quite invaluable as a companion." ("The Man with the Twisted Lip")

"I never get your limits, Watson . . . There are unexplored possibilities about you." ("The Sussex Vampire")

Holmes's softer side tended to emerge with the possibility of danger. When the two of them are off to burgle the home of Milverton the blackmailer . . .

"We have shared the same room for some years, and it would be amusing if we ended by sharing the same cell." ("Charles Augustus Milverton")

But his concern was really apparent when his own actions put his friend in mortal danger, as in the case of "The Devil's Foot."

"'Upon my word, Watson . . . I owe you both my thanks and an apology. It was an unjustifiable experiment even for oneself, and doubly so for a friend. I am really very sorry."

'You know,' I answered with some emotion, for I had never seen so much of Holmes's heart before, 'that it is my greatest joy and privilege to help you.'"

He relapsed at once into the half-humorous, half-cynical vein, which was his usual attitude to those about him.

"The view was sordid enough." (Sidney Paget for "The Naval Treaty," 1893)

And when Watson is shot and wounded by 'Killer' Evans in "The Three Garridebs" . . .

"'You're not hurt, Watson? For God's sake, say that you are not hurt!'

It was worth a wound—it was worth many wounds—to know the depth of loyalty and love which lay behind that cold mask. The clear, hard eyes were dimmed for a moment, and the firm lips were shaking. For the one and only time I caught a glimpse of a great heart as well as of a great brain. All my years of humble but single-minded service culminated in that moment of revelation.'It's nothing, Holmes. It's a mere scratch.'"

*　*　*　*

"Watson . . . you have never failed to play the game. I am sure you will play it to the end." ("The Mazarin Stone")

"We strolled about together." (Sidney Paget for "The Resident Patient,"
1893)

"His Last Bow"

"Come, friend Watson, the curtain rings up for the last act."

—"The Second Stain"

"The friends of Mr. Sherlock Holmes will be glad to learn that he is still alive and well, though somewhat crippled by occasional bouts of rheumatism. He has, for many years, lived in a small farm upon the Downs five miles from Eastbourne, where his time is divided between philosophy and agriculture. During this period of rest he has refused the most princely offers to take up various cases, having determined that his retirement was a permanent one."

—John H. Watson, MD

"I T'S SURELY time that I disappeared to that little farm of my dreams." ("The Creeping Man")

The latter part of Holmes's life has only fragmentary documentation. Watson—his 'Boswell'—had married again and moved

out of Baker Street for the last time and, although there is no reason to suppose he had lost either the desire or the ability to continue his narratives . . .

". . . the real reason lay in the reluctance which Mr. Holmes has
shown to the continued publication of his experiences. So long as he
was in actual professional practice the records of his successes were
of some practical value to him; but since he has definitely retired from
London, and betaken himself to study and bee-farming on the Sussex
Downs, notoriety has become hateful to him, and he has peremScoto-
rily requested that his wishes in this matter should be strictly
observed." ("The Second Stain")

In reading some of Watson's later accounts one can sense a
winding down, a deliberate final passage that seemed to parallel
the form of the music Holmes loved so much. There was, after all,
nothing left to prove, and perhaps he had proved himself right
once again—perhaps the days of the great cases *were* over.

In the latter part of June 1902 he "refused a knighthood for services which may perhaps some day be described"—but never were.

Then—in October of 1903—at the age of only forty-nine he
retired formally. He would speak of his "withdrawal to my little
Sussex home, when I had given myself up entirely to that soothing life
of Nature for which I had so often yearned during the long years spent
amid the gloom of London . . . My villa is situated upon the southern
slope of the Downs, commanding a great view of the Channel. At this
point the coast-line is entirely of chalk cliffs, which can only be
descended by a single, long, tortuous path, which is steep and slip-
pery. At the bottom of the path lie a hundred yards of pebbles and
shingle, even when the tide is full. Here and there, however, there are
curves and hollows which make splendid swimming-pools filled
afresh with each flow. This admirable beach extends for some miles in

each direction, save only at one point where the little cove and village of Fulworth break the line."

[Even now Holmes is carefully protecting his privacy. There is no village of Fulworth in Sussex.]

"My house is lonely. I, my old housekeeper, and my bees have the estate all to ourselves. Half a mile off, however, is Harold Stackhurst's well-known coaching establishment, The Gables."

Stackhurst had been "a well-known rowing Blue in his day and an excellent all-round scholar. He and I were always friendly from the day I came to the coast, and he was the one man who was on such terms with me that we could drop in on each other in the evenings without an invitation . . ." [A distinct sign of Holmes mellowing with age?] Stackpole was "a swimmer year round and, as I am a swimmer myself, I have often joined him."

One of those "splendid pools" in which they presumably swam was to be the setting for one final case—"The Lion's Mane" (1907)—which Holmes (in the absence of Watson) had to relate himself. ("In all my chronicles the reader will find no case that brought me so completely to the limit of my powers.")

"At this period of my life the good Watson had passed almost beyond my ken. An occasional weekend visit was the most I ever saw of him." And even those weekends must have become few and far between—or Watson's memory begun to have lapses—for him to be able to say, when they meet up a decade later . . .

"But you had retired, Holmes. We heard of you as living the life of a hermit among your bees and your books in a small farm upon the South Downs."

In fact, by this time Holmes had completed his definitive study of bees and was presumably still working on his (secret, unpublished) master work on detection "in a single volume."

* * * *

What brought the two old comrades together one last time was the biggest adventure of all and, although it was Holmes who made the running, it was only fitting that the faithful Watson should be there for the kill.

From the beginning of the century, relations between the various power centers of Europe had been markedly deteriorating. As far back as "The Naval Treaty" (1889) Prime Minister Lord Bellinger—"twice Premier of Britain . . . austere, high-nosed, eagle-eyed" —is warning Holmes about the sensitivity of the European situation and how the wording of the missing treaty could affect matters, if it became known to the wrong side . . .

"The whole of Europe is an armed camp. There is a double league which makes a fair balance of military power. Great Britain holds the scales. If Britain were driven into war with one confederacy, it would assure the supremacy of the other confederacy, whether they joined the war or not." ("The Second Stain")

[Bellinger is clearly a pseudonym for the Marquis of Salisbury—Robert Arthur Talbot Gascoyne Cecil (1830–1903), who was actually the Conservative Prime Minister on three separate occasions, in 1885, 1886–1891, and 1895–1902. In 1889 he would have been "twice Premier."]

Holmes, of course, retrieves the sensitive document and buys his country time but no more. The forces of disruption, led by Kaiser Wilhelm's Germany, are relentless and by mid-1914 feel ready to move against Britain.

Deep within the heart of British society, "like some wandering eagle," is Von Bork, "a man who could hardly be matched among all the devoted agents of the Kaiser. It was his talents that had first recommended him for the English mission, the most important mission of all, but since he had taken it over, those talents had become more and more manifest to the half-dozen people in the world who were really in touch with the truth."

On the eve of his departure for Germany and with the outbreak of World War I imminent, von Bork (with "his sunburned, aquiline face") confers with Baron von Herling, head of the German Legation in London. Von Herling congratulates him on the success of his longtime pose as "a born sportsman . . . you yacht against them, you hunt with them, you play polo, you match them in every game . . . What is the result? Nobody takes you seriously. You're 'a good sport,' 'quite a decent fellow for a German,' a hard-drinking, night club, knock-about-town, devil-may-care young fellow. And all the time . . . the sporting squire is the most astute Secret Service man in Europe."

It really has been all too easy. "The Brits . . . are not very hard to deceive. A more docile, simple folk could not be imagined," although von Herling cautions—"They have strange limits and one must learn to observe them. It is that surface simplicity of theirs which makes a trap for the stranger. One's first impression is that they are entirely soft. Then one comes suddenly upon something very hard and you know that you have reached the limit, and must adapt yourself to the fact. They have, for example, their insular conventions which simply must be observed . . . meaning British prejudice in all its queer manifestations."

But all of this is of no real concern, because the fact of the matter is "England is not ready . . . It is an inconceivable thing, but even our special war tax of fifty millions, which one would think made our purpose as clear as if we had advertised it on the front page of *The Times*, has not roused these people from their slumbers . . . as far as the essentials go—the storage of munitions, the preparation for submarine attack, the arrangements for making high explosives—

nothing is prepared. How then can England come in, especially when we have stirred up such a devil's brew of Irish civil war, window-breaking Furies, and God knows what to keep her thoughts at home?

"I fancy that in the future, we have our own very definite plans about England . . . It is today or tomorrow with Mr. John Bull . . . This week is their week of destiny . . . the heavens, too, may not be quite so peaceful if all that the good Zeppelin promises us comes true . . ."

At which point von Herling departs, leaving von Bork alone.

Shortly afterwards, he has two visitors. One is his chief agent, the Irish-American, Altamont, "a tall, gaunt man of sixty, with clear-cut features and a small goatee beard which gave him a general resemblance to the caricatures of Uncle Sam. A half-smoked, sodden cigar hung from the corner of his mouth." His companion and the driver of the "little Ford" car that brought them there—the only time Holmes is ever seen in a car—is "a heavily-built, elderly man with a grey moustache."

They are, of course, Sherlock Holmes and Doctor Watson, playing the roles of their lives. Before long they have the German safely trussed up and Holmes can explain his latest identity . . . "I started my pilgrimage at Chicago, graduated in an Irish secret society at Buffalo, gave serious trouble to the constabulary at Skibareen and so eventually caught the eye of a subordinate agent of von Bork, who recommended me as a likely man."

So completely had he become the character over time that von Bork can confidently describe him to von Herling as "a real bitter Irish-American (who) poses as a motor expert . . . He has a nice taste in wines and has taken a fancy to my Tokay." [The fact that it was Imperial Tokay from Franz Joseph's special cellar at the Schoenbrun Palace should perhaps have alerted anyone who had seriously studied his Holmes. When the encounter is safely over, he invites Watson to try this "remarkable wine," "Might I

"'Curse you, you double traitor!' cried the German, straining against his bonds and glaring murder from his furious eyes." (Albert Gilbert for "His Last Bow," 1917)

trouble you to open the window, for chloroform vapour does not help the palate."]

The job essentially over, Holmes turns to his old friend—"But you, Watson. How have the years used you? You look the same blithe boy as ever." [Watson was sixty-two at the time.]

Together at von Bork's cliff-top house overlooking the English Channel they take their last recorded bow.

For the last time they hear a defeated opponent curse and rail at the way he has been outwitted and promise revenge . . . "The old sweet song. How often have I heard it in days gone by. It was a favourite ditty of the late lamented Moriarty. Colonel Sebastian Moran has also been known to warble it. And yet I live and keep bees upon the South Downs . . ."

"Besides," he added not unkindly, as he laid his hand upon the shoulder of the prostrate man, "it is better than to fall before some more ignoble foe . . . The Englishman is a patient creature, but at present his temper is a little inflamed and it would be as well not to try him too far."

His thoughts then turn to wider issues. And for Holmes he becomes positively elegiac . . .

"'Stand with me here upon the terrace, for it may be the last quiet talk that we shall ever have. There's an east wind coming, Watson.'

'I think not, Holmes. It is very warm.'

'Good old Watson! You are the one fixed point in a changing age. There's an east wind coming all the same, such a wind as never blew on England yet. It will be cold and bitter, Watson, and a good many of us may wither before its blast. But it's God's own wind, nonetheless, and a cleaner, better, stronger land will lie in the sunshine when the storm has cleared.'"

As so often in the past, he was right.

What happened to the two of them, separately or together, may or may not have been recorded in Watson's tin dispatch box

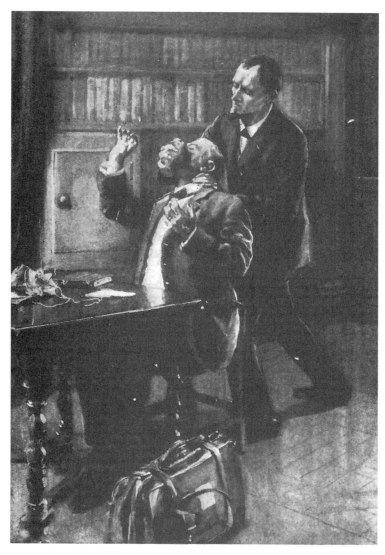

"He was gripped at the back of his neck by a grasp of iron, and a chloro-formed sponge was held in front of his writhing face."

Holmes as the double agent "Altamont" subdues Von Bork.

(Albert Gilbert for "His Last Bow," 1917)

in the vaults of Cox & Co. [The premises were bombed in World War II] Holmes is considered to have lived to 1957—thanks, presumably, to the benefits he derived from his advanced knowledge of apiculture. Watson—probably no thanks to the long-term effects of his war service—passed on in 1929.

We know that he enlisted again to serve as a surgeon in his old regiment in 1914 and must have seen sights that relegated even Maiwand into the shadows. After the 'war to end wars' he continued to chronicle their past cases until 1927—after which, honor served, the "tin dispatch box" found its way to Cox & Co.

By request there were no obituaries for either man.

All that can be said for sure is that neither of them withered before the storm and "a cleaner, better, stronger" England was the imperishable inheritance left behind by Mr. Sherlock Holmes and John H. Watson, M.D. (Late Indian Army).

*   *   *   *

"For England, home and beauty—eh, Watson?" [A traditional Royal Navy toast] ("The Bruce-Partington Plans")

OTHER TITLES OF INTEREST

THE SIR ARTHUR CONAN
DOYLE READER
From Sherlock Holmes
to Spiritualism
Edited by Jeffrey Meyers and
Valerie Meyers
592 pp., 1 b/w photo
0-8154-1202-9
$28.95 cl.

THE GERTRUDE STEIN
READER
The Great American Pioneer
of Avant-Garde Letters
Edited by Richard Kostelanetz
544 pp., 1 b/w illustration
0-8154-1238-X; 29.95 (cl.)
0-8154-1246-0; 19.95 (pb.)

THE H. G. WELLS READER
A Complete Anthology from
Science Fiction to Social Satire
Edited with an Introduction by
John Huntington
496 pp., 1 b/w illustration
0-87833-306-1
$19.95

THE GREENWICH
VILLAGE READER
Fiction, Poetry, and
Reminiscences, 1872–2002
Edited by June Skinner Sawyers
708 pp., 1 map
0-8154-1148-0
$35.00 cl.

AMERICAN WOMEN
ACTIVISTS' WRITINGS
An Anthology, 1637–2002
Edited by Kathryn Cullen-
DuPont
688 pp., 16 b/w photos
0-8154-1185-5
$37.95 cl.

ANNA WICKHAM
A Poet's Daring Life
Jennifer Vaughan Jones
344 pp., 30 b/w photos
1-56833-253-X
$26.95 cl.

THE COMPLETE
SHORT STORIES OF
MARCEL PROUST
Translated by Joachim
Neugroschel
Introduction by
Roger Shattuck
232 pp.
0-8154-1136-7; $25.95 (cl.)
0-8154-1264-9; $16.95 (pb.)

D. H. LAWRENCE
A Biography
Jeffrey Meyers
480 pp., 32 b/w photos
0-8154-1230-4
$18.95

EDGAR ALLAN POE
A Biography
Jeffrey Meyers
376 pp., 12 b/w photos
0-8154-1038-7
$18.95

ESSAYS OF THE MASTERS
Edited by Charles Neider
480 pp.
0-8154-1097-2
$18.95

THE FAIRY TALE
OF MY LIFE
An Autobiography
Hans Christian Andersen
New introduction by
Naomi Lewis
610 pp., 20 b/w illustrations
0-8154-1105-7
$22.95

GEORGE ELIOT
The Last Victorian
Kathryn Hughes
416 pp., 33 b/w illustrations
0-8154-1121-9
$19.95

GRANITE AND
RAINBOW
**The Hidden Life of
Virginia Woolf**
Mitchell Leaska
536 pp., 23 b/w photos
0-8154-1047-6
$18.95

GREAT SHORT STORIES
OF THE MASTERS
Edited with an introduction by
Charles Neider
576 pp.
0-8154-1253-3
$19.95

THE GROTTO BERG
Two Novellas
Charles Neider
Introduction by Clive Sinclair
184 pp.
0-8154-1123-5
$22.95 cl.

HEMINGWAY
Life into Art
Jeffrey Meyers
192 pp.
0-8154-1079-4
$27.95 cl.

JOSEPH CONRAD
A Biography
Jeffrey Meyers
464 pp., 32 b/w photos
0-8154-1112-X
$18.95

KATHERINE
MANSFIELD
A Darker View
Jeffrey Meyers
with a new introduction
344 pp., 29 b/w photos
0-8154-1197-9
$18.95

KEROUAC
The Definitive Biography
Paul Maher
Foreword by David Amram
512 pp., 24 b/w photos
0-87833-305-3
27.95 cl.

THE LANTERN-BEARERS
AND OTHER ESSAYS
Robert Louis Stevenson
Edited by Jeremy Treglown
320 pp., 27 b/w maps
0-8154-1012-3
$16.95

THE LIFE AND DEATH OF
YUKIO MISHIMA
Henry Scott Stokes
318 pp., 39 b/w illustrations
0-8154-1074-3
$18.95

LIFE AS I FIND IT
A Treasury of Mark Twain
Rarities
Edited by Charles Neider
with a new foreword
343 pp., 1 b/w photo
0-8154-1027-1
$17.95

LOVECRAFT AT LAST
H. P. Lovecraft and
Willis Conover
New introduction by S. T. Joshi
312 pp., 59 b/w illustrations
0-8154-1212-6
$29.95 cl.

MARK TWAIN:
PLYMOUTH ROCK
AND THE PILGRIMS
and Other Essays
Edited by Charles Neider
368 pp.
0-8154-1104-9
$17.95

O'NEILL
Son and Artist
Louis Scheaffer
750 pp., 71 b/w photos
0-8154-1244-4
$24.95

O'NEILL
Son and Playwright
Louis Scheaffer
544 pp., 62 b/w photos
0-8154-1243-6
$22.95

PLAYWRIGHTS ON
PLAYWRITING
From Ibsen to Ionesco
Edited by Toby Cole
Introduction by John Gassner
320 pp.
0-8154-1141-3
$18.95

SCOTT FITZGERALD
A Biography
Jeffrey Meyers
432 pp., 25 b/w photos
0-8154-1036-0
$18.95